mothers and daughters
at home

mothers and daughters

at home

35 projects
---
to make together

charlotte lyons

photographs by steven randazzo

SIMON & SCHUSTER

acknowledgments

Thank you to friends and family who have kept me on the pathway with encouraging assistance of all kinds: Anne and Jeff O'Connor, Michael Dinges, Nancy Drew, Elaine Kennelly, Jill and Rod Perth, Nan Morris, Nicki Dwyer, Barbara Martin, Kathy Brooks, Robyn D'Alba, Dede Thompson, Nan and Bob Ketcham, Elizabeth and Bruce Sperling, Kate Gangi, Lisa di Mona, Alison Cooper-Mullin, Lee Ann and Anne Marie Mercando, Nancy and Hali Schwartz, Kay Sorensen, Carroll Matthews, Charlie Manassa, Hans Viets, Mary Sue Voth, Susan Beach, and Mary Engelbreit.

Thank you to all who helped with the creation of the book: Colleen Mohyde, my delightfully enthusiastic agent; Constance Herndon at Simon & Schuster, for her commitment and intelligent guidance in bringing this idea to print, and Andrea Au, for all her hard work throughout; David Rosenthal, publisher, and Annik LaFarge, associate publisher, for their endorsement of the project; and also Jackie Seow, Peter McCulloch, Carrie Ross, and Beth Wareham; Steven Randazzo, who contributed an inspired dimension through his wonderful photography, and his assistants Ellie, Gene, and Michael; Mark Battrell for additional studio photography; Robin Winge at Winge & Associates, Inc., in Chicago, who brilliantly and thoughtfully designed this beautiful book, her assistant, Steve Wildi, for his dedication to the project, and Joel Heinz.

Special thanks to those who graciously permitted me to borrow their homes, faces, and stories for these pages: Jack and Chrissy Hurson; Barbara, Philip, Sara, and Ana Coccioletti; Jennifer, Jessie, and Casey Lambiase; Judy Plant and Brie Thompson; Myra Jane Sunderland; Dora Sperling; Erica, Chelseah, and Lauren Perth; Maggie O'Connor; Miriam and Bianca Hedges; Philip and Nan Coon; Brenda, Erin, and Whitney Christmas; Toni, Mary, and Kate Lydecker; Pat and Leah Schildknecht; Sally and Rachel Weaver; Diane and Alison Carter; Zoë and Ava Thompson; Sarah Najera; and Hayley Brooks.

Simon & Schuster
Rockefeller Center
1230 Avenue of the Americas
New York, NY 10020

Designed by Robin Winge
Winge & Associates, Inc., Chicago

Manufactured in the United States of America

10 9 8 7 6 5 4 3 2

Library of Congress Cataloging-in-Publication Data

Lyons, Charlotte.
    Mothers and daughters at home : 35 projects to make together / Charlotte Lyons ; with photographs by Steven Randazzo.
    p. cm.
    1. Handicraft. 2. Mothers and daughters. I. Title.
TT157.L97 2000
745.5—dc21   99-054522

ISBN 0-684-86273-5

For my mother, Charlotte O'Keefe, who showed me
the power of creativity with love, humor, and
confidence; my father, Bob Matthews, whose
cheerful appreciation makes all things possible;
my daughters, Erin, Maggie, and Maury,
whose dear gifts of spirit and enthusiasm
inspire my creative life; and especially my husband,
Andy, who knew wholeheartedly what
my dreams could become.

contents

introduction

She came into the kitchen with an enormous bunch of zinnias wrapped in newspaper, the magenta, crimson, and yellow blooms trailing out the top, water dripping from the stems in the coils of a pink rubber band. My mother grandly plunked them into a galvanized garden bucket on the counter and stood back to take in the startling mix of color and texture. "Aren't they gorgeous!" she exclaimed. "Look. I mean, really gorgeous?" she insisted. ◉◉ I was only ten and already an advanced student in style. Her style. ◉◉ It wasn't just the flowers and how pretty they looked on a hot summer day. It was the way she handled them, the choice she made to keep them in contrast to the newspaper, softly gray and smudged in the galvanized bucket, roughly battered.

THE MOTHER'S HEART IS THE CHILD'S SCHOOLROOM.

— HENRY WARD BEECHER —

effect. The look that is hers is now mine, too. And, like my mother, I love to make things for my home.

There were other lessons as well. My mother taught me how to sew, crochet, paint flea market furniture, decoupage, needlepoint, and whatever else she could think to do with her only daughter. These lessons were given in the spirit of fun and sharing. Some things we learned together, and some I taught her. Mostly, she emphasized the importance of home—the place itself mattered because we lived in it and we could make it our own with small gestures or grand plans.

This same experience has taken place in countless homes for generations. It is the centerpiece of the home I share with my husband and three daughters now.

> OF ALL THE RIGHTS
> OF WOMEN, THE GREATEST
> IS TO BE A MOTHER.
>
> — LIN YUTANG —

Though later stripped of the newspaper wrap, the zinnias stayed in the bucket on the counter for several days, the focus of small vignettes she built around them. A crystal candlestick and a blue-and-white porcelain platter pushed into place beside the bucket demanded that even I give it a glance as I ran past to dart outside. The next day a row of red tomatoes dotted the sill behind the bucket, crisply graphic trim interrupted by a small pottery bird that had been in the living room the day before. Like flash cards, these small still-life arrangements were my early lessons about scale, composition, and balance.

I did pay attention, it seems, because today my house looks very much like my mother's. There is a similarity of style, an imprint that is an inevitable result of my inspired admiration. The comfort upon which I thrived in her home is naturally what I aim to duplicate in my own. I am drawn to the same color of wood in a chest of drawers or the same patterns in a tapestry. I collect things like small pottery birds and invariably fall for old farmy buckets. When I bring them into my home, I know just where to put them for the right

Mothers and Daughters at Home examines and embraces the intimate personal style a mother shares with a daughter. The projects are not only fun and easy to do but produce excellent results that rival those found in shops or expensive boutiques. The most valuable element, however, is the shared experience of making something together. Inspired mothers and daughters will be delighted with their efforts as well as with the time spent at work with each other.

Busy as we are, we parents understand that childhood is a precious time with limited opportunities to really *be* with our children. So many things get in the way of spending time together in a meaningful way. We know that if we turn off the TV, computer, and headphones, we have to come up with something

pretty wonderful to keep their attention. Paintbrush, scissors, or needle in hand, I've never been turned down by any of my three daughters. At any age. Erin, my oldest, is twenty-one and still loves to take on a flea market transformation or a papier-mâché construction as long as it's going to her college apartment. My eighteen-year-old, Maggie, makes clever, original gifts for all members of the family and her lucky friends. Maury, who is twelve, comes up with wonderful project ideas and how-to techniques. Their efforts have blossomed in the appreciative environment of our home. They know that I love what they create and that they inspire my own creative life. I believe anyone can make beautiful and exciting accessories for the home with simple guidance and inspiration.

The projects we have made together in this collection include many popular home crafts such as quilting, decoupage, embroidery, papier-mâché, jewelry making, flea market transformations, doll making, and kitchen crafts. Several projects were inspired by the shared experiences of other mothers and daughters who have also discovered the instant and lasting rewards of working together. Profiles of these pairs underscore the emotional connection between working together and bonding mother to daughter, showing us how to create a

delightful experience with a loved one and wind up with a tangible family heirloom proudly displayed front and center, too.

You will find that many simple crafts can be adapted to use as mother-daughter projects. Choosing from chapters organized according to length of time and commitment, select from those projects best suited to your daughter's age, interest, and skill. Perhaps you have only an hour to spend with your daughter. There are several choices you can make that will fit the amount of time available and the range of your interests. The projects can be used as exact guides or as jumping-off points for different artistic adaptations. For instance, a young daughter might want to decorate a frame with glued-on rocks; an older daughter might prefer to use broken tiles or dishes. You may choose to cover yet another with silk flowers, or to make another version of your daughter's choice. Perhaps you will pursue a chance to craft a project with your own mother, who, like mine, still thinks it's fun to try something new. When we work together, the pleasure of that in itself makes the finished piece a kind of "party favor." Even the mistakes become cherished souvenirs of personal artistry and remembrance—made together as dearest friends, mothers and daughters. ❦

COLLAGED FRAMES

PAGE

14

DRAWSTRING BAGS

PAGE

18

DECORATED GIFT BOXES

PAGE

22

in an hour

Mothers become experts in using small pieces of time to accomplish all sorts of tasks that can otherwise fill a day. Busy lives mean fractured schedules of comings, goings, and doings for everyone. Opportunities to relax and have fun pop up unexpectedly in wee amounts also. ✕✕✕ Something else is always waiting in the wings, but an hour or so is all you might have today to share with your daughter. Look for a chance to call your own time-out and propose a project that's quick and easy.

YOU WILL NEVER "FIND" TIME FOR ANYTHING.
IF YOU WANT TIME, YOU MUST MAKE IT.

—CHARLES BUXTON—

DECOUPAGED BOTTLES

PAINTED NOTECARDS

PAINTED MUGS

APPLIQUÉD SWEATER

Time spent together making something is better than a rocking chair or a magazine, and it will refresh your spirit and hers. At the end of the day, this is the hour you will remember.

These projects can be made start to finish in one hour with any age daughter or mother, but that doesn't account for time spent collecting the materials. Take a minute to look over the projects and select those that seem most do-able for you. We all have different favorites when it comes to methods and style. Designate a special basket or drawer to fill with paper, fabric, paint, brushes, scissors, glue, bare wood frames, cookie cutters, and whatever else you will need. Make a quick list of things to have at hand to make your favorite and collect them now. Then when the time arrives—unexpectedly or by appointment, you will be all set to get on with the fun part. If you have a spare minute, put the teakettle on or maybe chill a pitcher of lemonade. Consider again that this is what you are doing to relax, to enjoy life, and to infuse it with memorable moments. This one is about sharing a precious part of your day with someone you love.

PAPER LACE

collaged frames

O ne of the easiest and most popular projects for the home begins with an inexpensive picture frame. To be able to combine a photograph of a loved one inside a homemade work of art is doubly pleasing. ◈◈◈ The frames can be ready-made from the department store or glued together from scraps found scavenging. Whatever your fancy, the project is easily adapted to any amount of creativity. The driftwood frames shown here came to be one summer at the beach. A scarcity of materials—white glue, driftwood, pebbles, and seashell fragments—yielded a primitive though sophisticated set of frames. ◈◈◈ Projects like these can be as basic as gluing twigs onto a cardboard rectangle or wrapping an old frame in cotton twine. Those collaged with themed junk and letter tiles (page 16) were the charming creations of then-seventeen-year-old Maggie. She surprised me with this set of three for Mother's Day.

WRINKLES SHOULD MERELY INDICATE WHERE SMILES HAVE BEEN.

— MARK TWAIN —

lthough it was not a project we did together, it didn't take me long to pick her creative mind for the how-to. The set on page 17 is a garage sale collection of peculiar tin trays that seemed to be good for something if we could just think of what that might be. Finally, we put them to use as impromptu frames. I like the way the images sit slightly askew inside. It makes me think of the business of life with kids—somehow it's much more interesting and exciting when it's a bit off-balance.

driftwood frames

Pictured on page 15

◆ **ARRANGE THE WOOD** lengths in a rectangular shape and glue together. Allow to dry undisturbed for thirty minutes to an hour. Arrange the decorations and glue into place with generous amounts of glue. Dry overnight. Hang with a nail at the top right and left inside corners for stability. Since there is no backing on the frame, use poster putty to stick photographs, postcards, or notes to the wall behind. If you prefer, glue the wood frame to the front of a purchased frame.

collaged set of three frames

Pictured below

◆ **THE GLUE GUN** allows you to work quickly, but it is hot and will burn little fingers (adult ones, too). For a young child, the white glue is a

better choice, but it must have time to dry. Check the backs of your frames to be sure hangers are where you want them. If they need to be attached, do so before you decorate the fronts. Center the letter tiles or beads on the top and glue into place. Arrange and glue the assorted beads, rings, or pennies into place all around. Generously cover the whole frame and build up the collage where needed to add interest.

frames out of trays

Pictured above

◆ MY FOUND TRAYS came with holes in them, but yours most likely will not. Find the center of the tray back just inside the raised edge that will now be the top of the frame. Use a drill or the awl and hammer to make a hole there. Thread the length of ribbon through the hole, through the button, and back through the button, and then once again through the hole in the tray. Tie off in a bow. Hang on the wall so that the bow conceals the nail hanger. Pull the button away from the tray just enough to slip a photograph or postcard beneath it. When you let go of the button and the ribbon, the tension creates a kind of clipboard to hold the image against the tray.

you will need

TO MAKE THE DRIFTWOOD FRAMES:
- 4 LENGTHS OF BROKEN ROUGH WOOD SUCH AS THESE STRIPS OF SAND FENCE
- ASSORTED SHELLS, ROCKS, PINE-CONES, OR OTHER NATURAL ACCENTS

TOOLS:
- WHITE GLUE, POSTER PUTTY, HAMMER AND NAILS

TO MAKE THE COLLAGED SET OF THREE FRAMES:
- 3 BARE WOOD FRAMES
- LETTER TILES FROM AN OLD BOARD GAME OR LETTER BEADS FROM A CRAFT STORE
- A BROKEN NECKLACE OF BEADS, SODA RING TOPS, PENNIES, BOTTLE CAPS, OR ANY OTHER CHARM YOU PREFER

TOOLS:
- HOT GLUE GUN AND GLUE STICKS, OR WHITE GLUE

TO MAKE THE FRAMES OUT OF TRAYS:
- SMALL WOODEN, PAPIER-MÂCHÉ, OR TIN TRAYS
- LARGE BUTTONS AND LENGTHS OF RIBBON

TOOLS:
- A DRILL, OR AN AWL AND A HAMMER

drawstring bags

Not long ago, my youngest, Maury, asked if she could learn to use the sewing machine. It isn't hard to operate, and she took to it easily. After sewing up and down on an old tea towel, she wanted more. Like driving a car, sewing isn't much fun without a destination. She wanted to go somewhere, to make something. ✖✖✖ So we cut two rectangles of fabric and began to sew up the sides. Down one long side, across the short, and back up the other long side. She did very well, and the seams were remarkably straight. A design decision presented itself. Close it up for a pillow or leave it open for a bag? ✖✖✖ A bag, the kind my grandmother would have called a ditty bag, took her fancy. It seemed much more fun to an eight-year-old than a pillow. She could put things in it, it would be useful. And it was already nearly complete.

HAPPINESS IS THE ABILITY TO RECOGNIZE IT.

— CAROLYN WELLS —

nce it was turned right side out, we threaded a length of thin, colorful ribbon through the top with a big embroidery needle, simply poking through the fabric at regular intervals to create a drawstring.

The next step called for some sort of decoration, which she added with a big floppy flower and stringy stem. Quite proud of her creation, she filled the bag with doll things and carted it around the neighborhood showing off her new sewing skills and nifty "ditty bag."

It wasn't long before her older sisters wanted their own—for travel, gift bags, and under-the-bed stowaway stuff. A cherished homemade doll dress was basted onto the front of one, another small bag took a cross-stitched initial, and a third became a canvas for a felt picture glued to the front. Flipping through magazines, textile books, or your own scrapbook of clips should provide ideas aplenty. As a final touch, a colorful ribbon and bow at the top make any effort look quite special.

✾ ✾ IN OUR EXPERIENCE it is easier to stitch decorations on the unconstructed pieces, which allows raw edges on the decorations to be sewn into the seams. If, however, you need to decorate after construction, it is certainly possible.

✾ ✾ AFTER CUTTING OUT two panels of fabric, choose one to be the front and apply the design (pattern on page 154) to this piece. You can hand-stitch, machine-sew, or glue the decoration into place, depending on your preference. If you choose to glue, allow plenty of time (about half an hour) for the glue to set. Then, with right sides together, sew the bag along the two sides and bottom. Turn right side out.

✾ ✾ FOLD DOWN the top edge if necessary and hemstitch for neatness. Fleece, like felt, does not need finishing. Burlap or other woven goods can be fringed or, if you plan ahead, you can use the factory-finished edge. Thread the drawstring through the bag a few inches below the top or simply fill the bag with desired contents and tie off with a bow.

you will need

TO MAKE THE FLEECE OR BURLAP BAG:
• 2 RECTANGLES OF FABRIC CUT
  TO A SIZE YOU PREFER:
  THE FLEECE BAG (CENTER) IS 10" x 16"
  THE BURLAP BAG (RIGHT) IS 6½" x 9"
• A LENGTH OF RIBBON FOR
  DRAWSTRING OR BOW TIE
• FLEECE AND FELT SCRAPS FOR
  DECORATION
TOOLS:
• WHITE GLUE OR NEEDLE AND THREAD

lucile, nan, and sarah

"Going away to college was the beginning of my own personal awakening to the many creative talents my mother, Lucile, possessed that were unique to her and not necessarily shared by every woman who had given birth," says Nan, recalling being stunned when a friend confided that her mother was incapable of sewing on a button. "In my mind that constituted some kind of terrible negligence. It even embarrassed me that someone should have to admit that.

THAT WAS A MOMENT of truth for me—that all mothers did *not* sew, knit, crochet, quilt, tailor, upholster, make slipcovers, make hats, paint fabrics, hammer copper. Because my mother did all that and plenty more. In our small town she availed herself of every possible class the vocational school had to offer, and she gave her daughters validity in the creative aspects of 'homemaking,' the major occupation of her generation. Through my own mother I think I have passed the creative interest gene to my daughter, Sarah, who has embraced it in her own way, and I am once again in awe of another talented woman seeking and finding creative fulfillment.

"I remember looking at Sarah's little hands once while she was cutting out paper dolls and thinking of that expression 'good with her hands.' I realized then that those small, lively fingers were one of Sarah's gifts. Her hands have always been quite nimble at doing things, making things. In a way, it was almost as if she was born to use them for intricate tasks. She cuts out tiny bits of beautiful paper or flowers and glues them together again into something unusual. I love to watch her decoupage a bowl or a gift box left behind, and I love it when she shows me how to try and do that, too." Nan laughs at herself, admitting that it is pretty hard to banish a persistent mother when she wants to join in.

Though paper dolls and puppets have had their turn, now Sarah is preparing for her wedding. "Sarah has thought of so many exceptional things to do for her wedding that will connect the two families and all the different friends between them. She really understands the importance of these personal touches. Designing and making the decorations and gifts for her bridesmaids is a wonderful way to share the meaning of the occasion. She has the spirit of my mother, and when she says 'I'm going to do this or that,' that's my cue to stick close. Believe me, I don't want to miss a thing."

ENTHUSIASM IS A
DIVINE POSSESSION.

———

MARGARET E.
SANGSTER

decorated gift boxes

This project could easily be modified for a different occasion or child's age. For instance, as a gift for a teacher, you might cover the box in a copy of a handprinted school alphabet or story. Decorate the top with a photograph of your daughter snipped from a copy of the class picture or perhaps her own self-portrait.

you will need

TO MAKE ONE BOX:

• A CARDBOARD GIFT BOX

• DECORATIVE PAPER OR A COPY OF
  AN INVITATION

• CUTOUTS FROM MAGAZINES,
  CATALOGS, OR GIFT WRAP

• PRESSED FLOWERS, IF DESIRED

TOOLS:

• SHARP SCISSORS, DECOUPAGE
  MEDIUM, AND A SMALL BRUSH

PLACE THE BOX TOP face-down on the wrong side of the decorative paper you have chosen for the backing. Trace around the top on the paper. Add a border that will allow the paper to wrap down and then back inside the side of the top. Cut it out. Apply decoupage medium to the box itself one part at a time and apply the precut paper as planned. Smooth out the wrinkles, bubbles, and edges. Set aside to dry. (This should take about fifteen minutes.)

For the wedding invitation box, add an overlay paper border made from carefully trimmed floral gift wrap. Apply these pieces with decoupage medium painted onto the backs of the paper cutouts. For smaller boxes, cover the box top with gold tissue paper and then add selected images themed to the occasion. For the pressed flower box, gently paint the backs of the pressed flowers with decoupage medium and place them onto the box top where desired.

Seal each box top with a coat of decoupage medium on all outside surfaces for a smooth, protected finish. Finish with a handmade gift tag made from the same decorative paper used on the box.

decoupaged bottles

All that business about those things that we learned in kindergarten serving us throughout our lives should really go a bit farther back to preschool. Preschool crafts lessons, that is. The projects my children did in preschool have kept us busy and happy for years and promise to do so well into the future. ᵠᵠᵠ This easy project is based on the popular preschool technique of picking through the trash, rescuing some overlooked resource, and giving it a new look with paste and paper. These decoupaged bottles and jars would be sweet place cards for a party. Decoupage a bottle for each guest with a photo of the guest or just a special name tag. Or fill the bottle with a lovely sprig of greenery or a flower stem and set it on the table as a bud vase. ᵠᵠᵠ Your guest can take it home; we also learned in preschool that there are few things as essential and gratifying as a party favor.

A CHILD'S ATTITUDE TOWARD EVERYTHING IS AN ARTIST'S ATTITUDE.

— WILLA CATHER —

BEGIN BY WASHING the bottles and jars and removing the labels or metal caps. We used a spaghetti sauce jar as well as juice and coffee drink bottles. Dry upside down on a rack to be sure the inside is dry, too. Choose the tissue paper you wish to cover it with—I use gold paper because it looks more sophisticated, but another color or pattern would be fine. Tear the tissue paper into small panels roughly the size of the bottle. Use the foam brush to paint the backs of the tissue shapes with decoupage medium. Put the pieces of tissue paper on the bottle and smooth them with the palm of your hand. The tissue papers go on very easily and conform to the glass shape nicely with a fair amount of smushing. Your preschooler will be very good at this part. Don't worry about the wrinkles; they're part of the look. If the edges aren't secure, slip some more glue beneath the paper and press again. Overlap as you like and cover the whole bottle in this way.

WHEN DRY (after ten minutes or so), paste the backs of the decorative cutouts and add as you would a sticker, being careful to press the edges down. If you have trouble getting stiff paper cutouts to conform to the rounded bottle shape, clip vents around the edges so that they flatten and smooth out more readily. Then paint the entire bottle with decoupage medium and allow to dry. Tie a raffia bow around the top and consider adding beads, acorns, or a tag to the raffia trim.

WE MADE THE NAME TAGS on the computer, although hand lettering would be fine. Trim the tag to size and finish off with an extra cutout decoration. In one case, the name tag became the bottle decoration itself. If cutouts are too much work to gather, consider using store-bought stickers. The fun is still there, and the project will go much faster.

you will need

TO MAKE A DECOUPAGED BOTTLE:
- AN EMPTY GLASS JAR OR DRINK BOTTLE
- TISSUE PAPER
- DECORATIVE CUTOUTS FROM CATALOGS OR MAGAZINES
- RAFFIA TRIM

TOOLS:
- DECOUPAGE MEDIUM, A FOAM BRUSH, AND SCISSORS

sally and rachel

Rachel inherited her mother's talent for art and then some. Through the years, Sally witnessed the willful momentum of her daughter's developing skill. She was delighted to see Rachel major in art in college and then receive her master's degree as well. Although Rachel lived away from home, they kept in touch by mailing little watercolor paintings back and forth to each other. These were small and simple pieces, sometimes meant for bookmarks or just something to tack onto the studio wall.

"MY STUDIO was Rachel's idea," Sally explains. "She understood my dream to devote more time to painting, so she told me to claim a spot in the house, get a comfy chair, and set up my easel. It was like we switched places. She even helped me pick out art books and things to fill the space for inspiration. Somehow art activities have been a common thread steadily weaving our lives together."

Like many mothers and daughters, though, there were times when personal issues created difficulties in communicating. Rachel, as a young woman, chose not to follow her mother's master plan. "She needed to be master of her own ship, and I still wanted to steer, which made it hard to be together. Then we arranged to meet on Saturday mornings for paint-at-my-house sessions that took the stress out of talking. It's easier to say things from behind an easel than from across the kitchen table. Art is such an equalizer, a very comforting way to be together. I am so grateful that we have that shared interest."

However, even in art they do not share a common style. Rachel had her own way of expressing herself from the start. "Rachel is very zany and experimental. I'm much more traditional. Sometimes we'll paint from the same still life and you'd never know we were looking at the same things."

Once Sally decided she would like to have a painted floor in their cottage dining room. She and Rachel decided a garden theme would look best, so Sally planned a grid of squares with diminutive perennial flower stems painted in each. One evening Sally returned home to find the floor half painted with voluminous blooms everywhere. Brush in hand, Rachel invited her mother to climb into the painted garden and get to work, too.

She did, of course, and many years later, Sally still enjoys her morning coffee in that room, where she can admire each power flower Rachel splashed onto the floor beside her own tidy sprigs, a warm memory and reminder of the creative dialogue between mother and daughter. "I'll have to keep this house forever, I guess," Sally says. "That floor is the most remarkable inspiration of all."

painted notecards

Sending a bit of yourself in the form of a card is a lovely way to keep the lines open. An inexpensive canvas board from the art supply shop can be painted and mailed in a padded envelope. Write the message right onto the back and off it goes. Lucky someone.

you will need

TO MAKE ONE NOTECARD:
- A 3″ x 5″ RECTANGLE OF FINE-QUALITY ARTIST'S PAPER, CANVAS PAPER, OR CANVAS BOARD
- A 4″ x 6″ OR LARGER FOLDED NOTECARD AND ENVELOPE

TOOLS:
- WATERCOLOR OR ACRYLIC PAINTS AND BRUSHES, PASTELS, OR COLORED PENCILS; DOUBLE-SIDED TAPE

FROM YOUR SCRAPBOOK of inspiration, select an image for your painting. It can be as simple as a tree, a heart, or a flower. A child's drawing often has the appeal of a museum piece, especially if the recipient is a biased grandparent or special friend. With the materials of your choice, paint the image onto the paper rectangle or canvas board. It is easiest to start with a small central image and then add borders or background patterns to build it out toward the edges. Or consider using the paper-lace technique in the next project for a card decoration.

WHEN FINISHED, use double-sided tape and mount the art to the front of the notecard. You could also cut out an opening in the card so that the painting is matted by the card front. This works well if you want to trim the image without cutting into it. Sign or initial the card front just below the art to make it a bit more special.

paper lace

A plain piece of paper and a good pair of scissors can amount to a great deal of pleasure and prettiness after snipping away a simple design. A snowflake, fold-out paper doll, or woodland scene can be mounted onto a backing paper and framed for keeps in an old frame. Measure the frame interior, then scale and cut the design to fit the opening. A paper box can also be decorated quickly with strong graphic images cut from paper. Try making greeting cards, scrapbook covers, and shelf trim this way. A young child will find that any crisp pattern created with the repeat images is successful. The trick is to go slowly and to let the scissors do their job. In some cases, a complex design is better handled with a craft knife and a cutting mat, although perhaps not with young children. Small pointed scissors are plenty sharp for most folded designs.

ADOPT THE PACE OF NATURE: HER SECRET IS PATIENCE.

— RALPH WALDO EMERSON —

you will need

to make a woodland scene

❧❧ ENLARGE AND TRACE the pattern from page 155 onto tracing paper. Fold the sheet of paper in half and transfer the traced pattern onto one half of the paper. Using sharp scissors, cut away the pattern along the lines drawn. Start in the center and move out to the edges. Turn the paper into the scissors to make smooth, even cuts. When finished, open the paper and place it flat between two pieces of paper to protect the work. Use the back of a spoon to press out the center fold. Clean any ragged cuts by trimming just the slightest bit. Spray the back with spray adhesive and apply to the backing paper, cut to fit the frame. Finish the framing and hang.

to decorate a bandbox

❧❧ PAINT THE BOX in the color of your choice and allow it to dry thoroughly. With the lid on the box, measure the height of the side to the lid and the exact circumference of the box. Cut a piece of paper to fit those measurements. If you must patch paper together to achieve the length you need, do that with glue before you begin to cut. Enlarge and trace the selected pattern from page 155 onto tracing paper, or make your own design and transfer to one end of the paper strip. Fold the paper accordion-style in segments that accommodate your pattern, being careful to keep the folds aligned.

❧❧ CUT OUT THE DESIGN. Unfold and place the strip between two pieces of paper to protect the work. Press out the creases with the back of the spoon. Use the hole punch to add details. Repeat this process to make a trim for the band around the lid, if you wish.

❧❧ TRACE THE TOP of the box onto a piece of white paper. Cut out this circle and cut away 1/2" all around to make it a little smaller. Fold as for a snowflake design—in half, then in quarters, with a sharp, pointed tip. Cut a design along the edges and then unfold. Use the spoon to press out the creases.

❧❧ WITH THE DECOUPAGE medium, paint the backs of the decorative pieces for the sides and top, and apply to the box carefully as planned. Smooth out the wrinkles gently. Most of the wrinkles take care of themselves while it dries, and you can press them again with the spoon back when it's dry. Then apply a coat of decoupage medium over all to seal the work.

paper and scissors

One of the most readily available materials today was not always so easy to come by. A luxury product to the early American colonists, paper was used sparingly and rarely by children, who practiced their schoolwork on reusable slates. In the eighteenth century, however, the French silhouette became a popular way of preserving family likenesses in profile and soon other paper-cutting styles followed. The German Fraktur, a paper design cut and delicately painted, was often used to create birth and wedding certificates. Many women took up the Scheren-schnitten technique of rendering detailed, symmetrical landscape scenes in cut paper.

ALL OF THESE STYLES crossed the Atlantic into the eager hands of American women looking for new ways to personalize their homes. Considered an excellent way to teach a child patience and care, these same crafts were soon being practiced by young girls at their mothers' side. Soon, making lacy fold-out valentines, decorative shelf trims, and paper dolls became a common pursuit.

Decoupage, a process of cutting and gluing decorative images into a new design on a functional background such as a tray or box, originated in France, where women had leisure hours to fill with the arts. Although widely admired as a decorative art, the craft really didn't flourish here until Victorian times, when women had more free time. With a few shortcuts, the enthusiastic decoupage artists in every household then began to decorate screens, boxes, and furniture with cutouts glued and varnished into place.

Paper chains at Christmas, valentines for a school class, snowflakes for the window, decoupaged treasure boxes, and other paper crafts have continued through the years. In the 1960s, I remember working with my mother on smaller versions of her project, decoupaging a greeting card cutout onto a wooden plaque. I'm sure her aim was to give me something to keep me busy so that she could make progress with her own work, but she always took the time to help me. Those brief lessons and my own discoveries fostered a growing creative interest. The tradition continues at my house. My daughter Maggie, once given a stack of colored paper and scissors to occupy herself while I worked, created a stunning cut paper design of African animals so remarkable that we took it to the local zoo. The art director purchased the design from Maggie, then age eleven, and silkscreened it onto hundreds of canvas bags for sale in the gift shop. I think my project that day went into the recycle bin, but what a great day for both of us!

appliquéd sweater

This sweetly decorated sweater can be made up quickly if you have the materials at hand. We had a plain sweater in a drawer and enough materials in the scrap basket to cut and stitch all the elements in an hour. This would make a delightful baby gift if your daughter has outgrown the stage of wearing such a young design—or you could do what I did and just hang it on the wall as a reminder of the days when she did.

you will need

TO DECORATE A SWEATER:

- A SWEATER WITH A PLAIN FRONT
- A LACY COLLAR TO ATTACH AROUND THE NECKLINE
- FELT OR FABRIC SCRAPS

TOOLS:

- PAPER FOR TEMPLATE, PINS, SCISSORS, NEEDLE, AND THREAD

BEFORE YOU ADD the design, loosely stitch the collar into place to see how it will change the remaining area of your sweater front. Draw the elements of your design (or ours from page 154) on a piece of stiff paper. Cut out the shapes for pattern templates. Pin these to the fabric pieces and cut them out. Arrange the design on the sweater front and pin it all into place.

Before you sew the pieces into place (the collar also), consider the look you want to achieve. If you use felt, the edges can be left unsewn and the center of a flower can be tacked securely for a floating, dimensional look. Cotton cut out with pinking shears could be treated the same way. I used a ribbed sweater cuff from another project to make a flowerpot that doubles as a tiny pocket. It is sewn in place along the bottom and sides, leaving the top open.

painted mugs

Acrylic paints have made a big dif-ference in the way we are able to craft at home. One of the nicest products to come onto the market was a paint that can be used on ceramics and glass, cleaned up with water, but becomes permanent when baked in the oven. It is a simple process that anyone can do in no time at all. The designs shown here (pattern on pages 154–155) are fairly simple but might not be as easy to render as larger fill-in shapes such as flowers, polka dots, or just plain stripes. An extra coat of paint gives most designs added strength in color and stroke, but if it isn't what you hoped for, just wash it away and try again.

✿ BEGIN WITH A VERY CLEAN MUG or cup. Draw your design on with a pencil or marker, if you choose, or just paint it right onto the mug. The colors can be mixed for a variety of shades, so make several small pools of paint colors to choose from and mix the others out of these. We use a paper plate or a sheet of wax paper for this so that it can just be thrown away afterward. A plastic drink cup is the best holder for water to clean the brushes with between colors, and paper towels are a must.

✿ APPLY THE PAINT to the cup front without getting too close to the upper edge. The cotton swabs come in handy for delicate touch-ups or for wiping away unwanted paint strokes. When you are happy with the design, allow the paint to dry (about ten to fifteen minutes) and then follow the manufac-turer's instructions for baking or air drying to cure. Also, note whether your paint is dishwasher proof. Otherwise hand wash. Lastly, be sure to clean the brushes thoroughly with soapy warm water and air dry, tips up.

you will need

TO MAKE PAINTED MUGS:
• PLAIN CHINA OR GLASS MUGS
• ACRYLIC PERMANENT PAINTS
  (COLORS CAN BE MIXED)
TOOLS:
• BRUSHES AND COTTON SWABS, AN
  OVEN TO BAKE THE FINISHED MUG

KEEPSAKE PINS

PAGE

40

BUTTON NECKLACE

PAGE

44

TEA COZY

PAGE

50

half a day

If you have a good supply of materials at hand, half a day can be enough time to create something quite exceptional together. This is time enough to bake, stitch, or daydream and create the possibilities, too. Half a day disappears in a wink, though, so be prepared. When your daughter is little and off to school for a half day,

put that time to use planning the project. Imagine her excitement when she realizes you have something special for the two of you to do together.

OPTIMISM: A CHEERFUL FRAME OF MIND THAT ENABLES A
TEAKETTLE TO SING THOUGH IN HOT WATER UP TO ITS NOSE.

— ANONYMOUS —

CARAMEL ROLLS

PAGE

54

EVERLASTING WREATH

PAGE

62

COOKIE CANDLE BOX

PAGE

66

GOOD CHEER FAIRY

PAGE 46

If you have the tools and materials, or just an idea for inspiration, you can make something together that creates a special memory to share later.

These projects can be made in a single morning or afternoon, but your priority should be the pleasure more than the project. The pace you establish should be one that allows you to be relaxed, at your best, and truly creative. If you finish the project quickly and have a bit more time, you could make another version of your own design or create one for a gift. You might make something together that could be donated to a charity such as a school fundraiser. Once you learn a technique, repeating the process is so much more enjoyable.

Taking a break every now and then is a good idea, too. Stand back and admire your work, straighten up the table some. Tell a funny story about something you made when you were little. Perhaps the project happens to take you longer than expected. Leave it out where you will be tempted to take it up again.

Don't hesitate to let the experience spill over into the next day. This kind of fun and shared pleasure can be unstoppable. What better sign of success is there than the wish to continue?

DECOUPAGED STEPSTOOL

PAGE 58

keepsake pins

After an evening spent browsing through old family photo albums, Maggie and I were inspired by the sweet young faces and the good old days to make the most of our dear relatives. ⊙⊙⊙ Enticing pieces of jewelry like these photo pins can be found in expensive shops, but they are fairly simple to make. Although they can be fashioned entirely out of materials available at the craft shop, we also had good luck with some pieces of broken jewelry that were incorporated into the project. The bird pin was missing the charm that once hung from the bottom, but the charm was easy to restore with a jump ring, pliers, and a newly assembled photo frame. ⊙⊙⊙ As a variation, consider making one large enough to hang on the wall as a framed work of art, or perhaps mount it inside a small memory box. Another way to use this is as a cover on a photo album or family scrapbook.

CHEERFUL PEOPLE LIVE LONGEST HERE ON EARTH,

AFTERWARD IN OUR HEARTS.

— ANONYMOUS —

you will need

TO MAKE ONE PIN:

- A CLEAR PHOTOCOPY OF A PHOTOGRAPH WITH THE MAIN IMAGE MEASURING LESS THAN 1″ HIGH (YOU CAN REDUCE A COLOR PHOTO ON A BLACK-AND-WHITE COPY MACHINE)
- A SMALL PIECE OF CARDBOARD OR MAT BOARD FOR THE BACKING
- A CRAFTER'S FRAME FROM THE JEWELRY CHARM DEPARTMENT
- A SMALL SQUARE OF ACETATE (ART STORE) THAT FITS THE FRAME
- BUTTONS, CHARMS, RIBBONS, SILK FLOWERS, AND PIN BACK AND JUMP RINGS

TOOLS:

- WHITE GLUE, NEEDLE-NOSE PLIERS, AND A CRAFT KNIFE

⊚⊚ CENTER THE FRAME over the best part of your photocopy. Trace around the outside of the frame to fit the copy. Do the same for the acetate. Cut out both pieces. Fit the acetate over the image, then gently fit it into the frame. This frame came with a backing, so we used the pliers to close the frame back securely. For the bird pin, there wasn't much more to do; we simply attached the frame to the bottom with a jump ring.

⊚⊚ TO MAKE THE RIBBON-and-fabric frame, we completed the frame and placed it on top of the cardboard piece. If you intend to wear it, keep the overall size on the small side. This one is 3″ long and 1 1/4″ wide. Arrange the buttons, flowers, and lace or charms in a pleasing design around the frame while it's resting on the cardboard. We covered the cardboard back with fabric, adding a ribbon bow and antique button. If you are attaching a hanging charm, as we did, do so with pliers and a jump ring before you glue all the elements together. Glue the decorations and assembled frame to the cardboard back and allow to dry. Later, when all is dry (it will take about an hour), glue a pin back to the cardboard back.

books and ornaments

⊚⊚ IF THE IMAGE is larger, it might be lovely as an ornament or on a book cover. I used the copier to reduce a picture of my father for a journal cover. A short length of ribbon, some rick rack, and a favorite button were glued onto the board backing for decoration.

diane and alison

Diane seemed to be spending an awful lot of time driving her daughter, Alison, to shows—bead shows, where Alison spent all her energy and all her baby-sitting money in the way most teens shopped for clothes. Wandering around the big halls trying to keep track of Alison's excited interest as she flitted from one vendor to another, Diane didn't really get it until she began to look at the wares themselves. Lambent pools of candy-colored glass baubles in pots and baskets, begging to be touched. Glazed clay rounds, ancient tribal icons inscribed on their edges. Loopy strings of eclectic ornaments to entice the collector or the artisan. The beads were, indeed, mesmerizing.

IF A CHILD

LIVES WITH APPROVAL,

SHE LEARNS TO

LIKE HERSELF.

———

DOROTHY

LAW NOLTE

AT HOME, Alison retreated and spent hours sifting through her carefully chosen beads, sorting them and then stringing them into fanciful creations that gave everyone, especially Alison, enormous pleasure. "I never really thought of myself as one who was good with a needle and thread even though my own mother worked for a milliner and made beautiful things," Diane confesses. "But one day I borrowed inspiration from Alison and signed up for a beading class at the local bead shop. I was curious and that's all it took. I was hooked right away."

These days, Diane is the one logging the shows onto the calendar and collecting beads by the bagful. With Alison's encouragement, Diane has caught up to her daughter's skill level with a similar enthusiasm and a style all her own. She is grateful for the new creative awareness Alison introduced into both their lives. Now that Alison is away at college, Diane feels as though they are somehow connected in spite of the distances, knowing that they are both thinking in the same language of craftsmanship.

Alison is as proud of her mother's work as she is of her own. "When I was a kid in junior high it made me feel so important to have her ask my advice about a bead or a pattern. We really started to be friends with this, and then artistic partners, too. I feel like Mom includes me in so much of her work, inviting my input with decisions along the way. It's really important to have someone else give you feedback. Mom and I are very honest in our exchange of criticism and praise.

"When my friends come over and see what Mom has made, a little of my pride is that I feel a part of her work. She makes beautiful things that always impress me and feed my own interest. I don't think we'll ever stop doing this, individually or together, but I might have if she hadn't joined me. I probably would have given up long ago, if not for her. It's come to be a very strong bond between us."

button necklace

Every once in a while, a simple object can inspire others to follow. I was lucky enough to discover in a thrift shop a necklace that appeared to be pearls. Closer inspection showed that it was made from handmade pearl buttons sewn to a length of crocheted trim. I imagine someone like me thought the buttons too pretty to hide on a dress and instead fashioned this lovely choker to make the most of her treasured "pearls." We used the same idea to make our own. Having an abundance of fancy trims and buttons on hand shortened the process, although the pleasure of mixing and matching can take up an afternoon in itself.

BEGIN BY EXPERIMENTING with the choices and combinations that look best on the ribbon trim you have selected. Once an arrangement is established, sketch it on a piece of paper. I wanted my leaf button to hang as though it were a pendant, so I used a loose sewing stitch to attach it to the ribbon and then fortified the thread with a repeated wrap stitch around the hanging loop. I also sewed a second, small button over the leaf button hole to conceal it and add more decoration. On the

ribbon trim above, I added another favorite button with a bird to conceal the rest of the thread loop. Since the trim was fairly elegant, the simple flower buttons seemed enough ornament. The plastic flower buttons were originally a dull tan color, so I painted them first with an acrylic antique gold paint.

To finish the necklace, attach jewelry findings to the ends, or fold and stitch one end back on itself to create a buttonhole and then attach extra buttons to the other end for an adjustable fit.

you will need

TO MAKE ONE NECKLACE:
- A PROMINENT CENTER BUTTON
- AN EVEN NUMBER OF SMALLER
  BUTTONS TO COMPLEMENT THE FIRST
- 18″ DECORATIVE RIBBON OR TRIM
- JEWELRY CLOSINGS

TOOLS:
- NEEDLE AND STRONG THREAD
  TO MATCH THE RIBBON

good cheer fairy

This little fairy doll requires the littlest amounts of fabrics and trim. If you have ever saved a scrap of pretty ribbon, a wee square of vintage fabric, or a favorite button, this is the time to use it up. As a gift, the 6″ fairy conveys whatever message you want to send: get well, sympathy, hugs and kisses, friendship. ✷✷✷ Think of ways to add your own details. Perhaps she should have yarn hair or carry a basket with a secret message tucked inside. How might you make a wand out of a toothpick, a twig, or a straw? ✷✷✷ Once finished, she is meant to float from a bedpost or cupboard latch as a reminder to chin up for good cheer and sunshine.

KEEP YOUR FACE TO THE SUNSHINE AND
YOU CANNOT SEE THE SHADOW.

— HELEN KELLER —

you will need

TO MAKE ONE FAIRY:

- 2 PIECES OF MUSLIN 7″ x 8″
- POLYESTER STUFFING
- ACRYLIC PAINTS: WHITE, BRICK RED, BLACK
- DOLL HAT 2″ IN DIAMETER
- 18″ WIRE-EDGED RIBBON
- 10″ x 5″ RECTANGLE OF FABRIC
- CRAFT FLOWERS, MINI CLAY POT, AND FLORAL CLAY
- THIN-GAUGE BEADING WIRE AND WRAPPED FLORAL WIRE
- LACE FOR COLLAR
- BUTTON
- BUNDLE OF RAFFIA CUT TO 6″ LENGTH

TOOLS:

- SCISSORS, SEWING MACHINE, NEEDLE AND THREAD, FINE-TIPPED BRUSHES

✲✲ ENLARGE AND DRAW the pattern from page 154 onto the muslin and stitch the two body pieces right sides together (it's best to use a sewing machine), leaving an opening in the middle of one side. Trim close to stitching and clip inner curves at the arms, neck, and legs. Turn inside out, using the eraser end of a pencil to fully turn the arms and legs. Stuff lightly, leaving shoulder joints loose, and stitch the opening closed.

✲✲ TRY THE HAT ON to see where it comes down on the face. Set hat aside. Paint on the face according to this adjustment. Paint the general face area in a background color of your choice. Mix a touch of white into black to make a charcoal-hued paint for eyes and nose. Use the smallest bit of paint for these features. Use the brick red for the mouth and add white to remaining red paint for pink blushes at the cheeks. Smudge these with a cotton swab for subtlety.

✲✲ FOLD THE RECTANGLE of dress fabric in half and snip a 3/4″ neck opening in the center of the fold with a 1/2″ slit opening down the back (resembles a T). Put the dress on the doll poncho-style and use sewing thread to gather it slightly around the middle under the arms. It is meant to be rather primitive, so don't fuss over this too much or finish the raw edges. Cinch it with a raffia belt and a button for the buckle. A bit of lace glued to the neckline makes a collar and provides a clean finish at the neck. Decorate the hat before you put it on the doll. Then glue it to her head at the top. If you like, you could add a shank of yarn or twine hair beneath the hat before you glue it on. Keep the brim low over her eyes.

✲✲ CUT A SHANK of raffia for wings and tie it in the middle with a loose piece of raffia. Trim the edges of the wings to be even and sew the bundle to the back of the doll securely. If you prefer, you might use a paper doily for the same effect. Pinch it in the middle as you would if you were making a butterfly's wings and sew it in place at the gather. Put a plug of floral clay into a miniature clay pot (dollhouse accessories) and "plant" it with silk posies cut to fit. Use beading wire to rim the pot and thread the wire through the inside palms of the fabric hands of the doll, drawing them together as though she is holding the pot. Twist and snip the wire behind her hands.

✲✲ AT THE BACK of the doll, thread a 12″ floral wire hanger through the dress above the wings and twist shut for a hanger or use another length of raffia for a hanging loop. If the doll will be a gift, a small handwritten tag can be added to the hands with a length of raffia. Copy a favorite quote onto the back of the tag.

doll making

Before toy stores and mail-order catalogs, most dolls and toys were made by hand at home out of materials available indoors and out. A wishful child might present her mother with a handful of worn household fabrics and a scrap of lace in the hope that her mother would have time to transform the bundle into a doll. Perhaps the head would be fashioned from a hickory nut, a dried apple, or a corncob.

FABRIC, PAPER, WOOD, papier-mâché, clay, and wax were traditional favorites for dollmakers. Indeed, women have made dolls for their daughters out of just about anything that was available to them. In the spirit of resourcefulness and pleasure, a doll made of a few twigs wrapped together with wildflower stems, dressed in spring leaves, and wearing a dandelion hat might inspire hours of imaginative independent play. Scraps from the rag bag were often stitched together between other tasks of a busy day to make the dearest doll or stuffed animal, especially if it was made by Mother and given with a homespun story. Topsy-turvy dolls, pocket dolls for quiet play in church, and the devoted teddy bear are magical gifts of affection that make the most out of honest, humble beginnings.

Dolls and stuffed animal toys are part of every culture in the world. In ancient Egypt dolls were made from linen, stuffed with papyrus, and embroidered. Dolls and toys have been designed and used throughout history to teach folklore, legends, and lessons. Additionally, a doll carries with it a unique tradition of craftsmanship and style usually representative of a culture, a region, or a family. Few children ever give up a doll or a bear, even as adults, because it was both a treasured companion and a prized responsibility. Though the toys themselves were created simply to give pleasure and encourage imaginative play, much of a child's play naturally centered on the business of mothering, the daily tasks and responsibilities of running a household and raising children. A daughter might learn to sew in an effort to make new clothes for her doll or perhaps to patch and quilt a bed covering for her. She learned to be clever and resourceful like her mother as well as kind, sympathetic, and gentle.

tea cozy

others of little girls know that it is but a short step from a pot of tea to an all-out party. With this in mind, I have always kept a drawer in the kitchen reserved for all the elements of an impromptu tea party. A special cloth for the table (one that does not require ironing or worrying over), cloth napkins, and a tea cozy are ready and waiting for the moment to arrive. ◉◉◉ Tea with dolls and small children can fill an entire afternoon, and tea that begins just barely warm for safety cools quickly. Having a thick tea cozy for the pot delays the chill while also providing extra protection for a china pot that will be handled briskly by excited children. ◉◉◉ Our teapot isn't all that special, but I know three girls who will ask for it years from now. We have treated it with care from the start. This cozy is simple to make using old sweaters, which seems most appropriate for this project —a sweater for a teapot.

TO HAVE JOY ONE MUST SHARE IT. HAPPINESS WAS BORN A TWIN.

— LORD BYRON —

◉◉ BEGIN BY WASHING the sweaters in hot water to felt them and then place them in the dryer (see Glossary). Enlarge and trace the tea cozy pattern from page 156 to paper and pin the paper to the prepared sweaters. Cut out the two sides and repeat for the lining. Cut out the bottom piece. We chose to make the outside in two different colors, but it isn't necessary to do so.

◉◉ CUT OUT THE DECORATIVE pieces from the patterns and pin them to the cozy sides. Using sewing thread in a contrasting color, stitch them into place. We used a big whipstitch that laced each vine into place and then added leaves and flowers in the same way. For an inexperienced sewer, this method goes quickly and is easy to manage, thanks to the wool, which does not require that the edges be finished and forgives all manner of mistakes. The stitches sink into the wool a bit so that just the dashes of colored thread show.

- - - - - -

Have a small wrapped gift waiting

for your daughter or mother

when she joins you for time together.

A personal sewing kit, a set of brushes,

a favorite book, or a family treasure can set

the tone for a special day. Is this

a good day to give your daughter

Grandmother's teapot?

- - - - - -

you will need

————

FOR A TEA COZY SIZED TO FIT A 7″ TEAPOT:
• 2 OR 3 LIGHTWEIGHT WOOL SWEATERS IN COLORS SUCH AS BLUE, TURQUOISE, AND GREEN
• SCRAPS OF SWEATERS OR WOOL FELT IN PALE BLUE, TURQUOISE, LAVENDER, AND CORAL
TOOLS:
• SCISSORS, SEWING THREAD, AND A NEEDLE
• PINS

◉◉ BACK EACH DECORATED tea cozy side with a lining piece and sew the edges together using blanket stitches, leaving an opening at the left side of one piece and the right side of the other for the elastic band. Cut a 16″ × 2″ piece from the ribbed band of one of the sweaters (ribbing is more elastic) and fold it in half lengthwise. Stitch it lengthwise with loose blanket stitches and insert the two ends into the two openings at the sides of the cozy. Stitch the openings securely closed. Right sides together, pin and sew in the bottom round with hemstitch. Turn.

◉◉ TO PLACE ON THE TEAPOT, open the cozy, set the pot inside, and pull the sides up around the pot so that the spout comes out of one side opening and the handle out the other. Twist the band once and stretch over the gathered tea cozy top. Twist the band again and stretch it back over the top once more.

caramel rolls

Somehow these gooey rolls always come out of the oven just in time for tea. Of course, teatime could be any time at our house depending upon what is coming out of the oven. ❦ ❦ ❦ This recipe makes two cakelike rounds—enough to share with a neighbor, grandparent, school bake sale, or a friend. ❦ ❦ ❦ Baking bread is a wonderful experience to share with a child. Hands full of flour kneading deep into the dough, a child feels genuinely in charge of something especially important. ❦ ❦ ❦ The process of dough rising into new forms is also a thrill, and slicing the rolled dough into even portions is a nice way to teach fractions.

ONE OF THE SECRETS OF A HAPPY LIFE IS SMALL TREATS.

— IRIS MURDOCH —

you will need

TO MAKE TWO LOAVES OF
TWELVE ROLLS EACH:

- 1 CUP MILK
- 1/4 CUP SUGAR
- 1/4 CUP BUTTER
- 1 TSP. SALT
- 1 PACKAGE ACTIVE DRY YEAST
- 3 1/2 CUPS FLOUR
- 2 EGGS
- 2/3 CUP GRANULATED SUGAR
- 2 1/2 TSP. CINNAMON
- 1 STICK BUTTER
- 2/3 CUP BROWN SUGAR
- 2 TABLESPOONS LIGHT CORN SYRUP
- 1 CUP CHOPPED WALNUTS
  OR PECANS

IN A POT on the stove or in the microwave, heat the milk, 1/4 cup sugar, 1/4 cup butter, and salt until very warm. Stir the mixture to melt the butter completely. In a large mixing bowl, combine the yeast with 1 1/2 cups of the flour. Add the milk mixture while warm (120° for this type of yeast: if the liquid is too cool it will not activate the yeast; if it's too hot it will kill it and prevent the dough from rising) and blend with a wooden spoon.

Add both eggs. Using the electric mixer, beat three minutes on high. Add the remaining 2 cups of flour and mix by hand. Turn out onto a floured board and knead eight minutes, until the dough takes on a smooth consistency.

Occasionally raise the dough about ten inches from the board and drop forcefully onto the board. Guess who will want to help with this part? Continue kneading using the heels of your hands, turning the dough inside out with the push and pull of this process.

WASH OUT THE BOWL and dry it, then spray heavily with cooking spray. Put the dough back into the bowl and turn it over so that the top is greased also. Cover with a damp towel and allow to rise in a warm, draft-free place. I place mine in an oven that has been warmed briefly (turn it on at 200° for five minutes and then turn it off).

Let the dough rise one hour or so, until doubled. Punch it down in the center and divide it in half with a knife. Let it rest for a few minutes while you prepare the cinnamon sugar and caramel mixture.

MIX 2/3 CUP GRANULATED sugar with 2 1/2 teaspoons cinnamon. Set aside. Melt 1 stick butter and pour 1/4 cup into a small dish to set aside. Add 2/3 cup brown sugar to remaining butter in the pan and add 2 tablespoons corn syrup.

☆ **TAKE HALF THE DOUGH,** shape into a rough rectangle, and use a rolling pin to roll out into a rectangle approximately 12″ × 8″. Brush with half the reserved butter. Sprinkle with half the cinnamon-sugar. Starting at one long side, roll the dough jelly roll fashion.

Cut the roll into twelve equal pieces (halves, each half in half again, then each quarter into thirds).

Into a 9″ cake pan, pour half the brown sugar mixture and spread evenly in the pan. Sprinkle half the chopped nuts onto this and then place the cut rolls, cut side down, onto the mixture. Place them evenly spaced, with eight around the outside and four in the center. They will rise later so that their sides touch, forming a round cake. Repeat with the second half of the dough and the remaining ingredients to make a second cake in another pan. Cover each pan with a damp towel and allow to rise a second time for about thirty to forty-five minutes.

☆ **REMOVE THE TOWELS** and bake in a preheated 375° oven for eighteen minutes, until golden brown. Cool ten minutes and then turn upside down onto a plate so the sugared, nutty side is on top. Eat them right away for the best sweet roll experience.

* * *

CREATE A RECIPE

SCRAPBOOK

These caramel rolls might surely be an addition to your Recipe Scrapbook (*Chapter Five*). Let your daughter decorate the page herself. It will capture her youthful spirit and imagination along with the recipe for a lifetime of memories.

decoupaged stepstool

Many years ago, I was given a shovelful of earth with the promise that it held a fern root. "Stick it in your garden," my friend advised. "Then the fairies will live there." ❧ ❧ ❧ I don't think I ever saw any fairies, but the ferns were an extraordinary pleasure every spring, arching and unfurling their luminous fronds like tiny starched sails. Before summer scorched the delicate stems last year, the girls and I picked a few fronds and pressed them in a book along with pansies and flax blossoms. ❧ ❧ ❧ Much later, when it was time to decoupage this rummage sale stepstool, we opened the book, pleased to see that the crisp little fern fronds looked quite elegant still. Thanks to the color copier, we could have our fern and decoupage it, too. Even better, when placed onto the copier with the illustrated page behind it, we did not have to cut out the fern—we decoupaged the whole page.

ALL THINGS ARE POSSIBLE UNTIL THEY ARE PROVED IMPOSSIBLE—
AND EVEN THE IMPOSSIBLE MAY ONLY BE SO, AS OF NOW.

— PEARL S. BUCK —

A collection of colored butterflies and a vintage postcard, photocopied also, provided the rest of the images we would need. As with most projects, fooling around with possibilities took the most time here. For me, though, that creative brainstorming is the best part.

❧❧ THIS RUMMAGE SALE stepstool had a certain charm of its own that dictated the design of the decoupage. We didn't want to obscure any of the old painted finish, so we stayed true to the vintage feeling it already had when choosing images. When finished, it looked as though it still belonged in some old farmy kitchen where you could look out the window and see the very same butterflies, birds, and ferns in the garden. But it did need to be washed and sanded first to remove dirt and loose paint. When you are sure that your stepstool is well prepared, seal the surfaces with acrylic sealer.

❧❧ ARRANGE THE IMAGES on the seat top. Trace around their edges lightly with a pencil for placement markers to refer to later. Beginning with the base piece, paint the back of the paper with decoupage medium and apply it to the seat. Smooth with your fingers to get the bubbles out and allow to dry before layering another image on top. When dry (after about fifteen minutes), proceed with the other images. We accented parts of the printed page with strokes of white paint and a wash of weak coffee to add an interesting patina to the paper. When everything is dry and finished to your liking, seal the seat with three coats of acrylic sealer.

you will need

TO DECOUPAGE THE TOP OF
A STEPSTOOL:
• A PAINTED OR NATURAL SEALED
  STEPSTOOL
• IMAGES TO CLIP OR COPY
• WEAK COFFEE AND WHITE PAINT
• ACRYLIC SEALER
• DECOUPAGE MEDIUM
TOOLS:
• SCISSORS, SANDPAPER, AND
  FOAM BRUSH

dede, zoë, and ava

Dede loves to work on home craft projects. She makes scrapbooks, and she decoupages and paints. The mother of two daughters, eleven and six, she cherishes these undertakings as personal getaways where she can lose herself in the project and explore a creative life that is a kind of meditation. Her daughters, Zoë and Ava, love what she makes and see how much pleasure and pride crafting gives her. They want to do that, too.

A MOTHER IS NOT
A PERSON TO LEAN ON,
BUT A PERSON TO MAKE
LEANING UNNECESSARY.

———

DOROTHY CANFIELD
FISHER

"IT'S A WONDERFUL THING to find something to share with your children that you can do together, and I appreciate everything that it means to work together. But since I have so little time to work alone it becomes really precious. There are invariably moments when I'm immersed in a project and suddenly Ava discovers me at a point when the work looks very inviting. Of course, she wants to join in. Heads up! She's six, and it's going to be a different experience now. It's hard to stop midway through a project and start from the beginning again, so I have spent some time teaching both girls to be independently creative with their own materials, space, and responsibility for the process. I'm there to help where I can and share the fun, but I try to excuse myself from the creative equation."

That also means holding back any criticism that would stifle that experimental effort. For Dede, this is about developing the habits of commitment to the creative process; the concept, the work, the problem solving, and the evaluation should belong to the child. "The skills come along with age and experience. To see something you love started up in your daughter is exciting, but is such a fragile thing. Praise the way she handles the process by saying 'I really like the way you did this,' because it builds the independence and confidence to work on her own. Most of the things I make, I give away to friends or family—a good tradition to establish for a child as well, and it brings heaps of praise and appreciation from another voice. For Christmas this year Zoë made a decoupaged box for me. It was so touching to see how much it meant to her to tackle this craft that I love and proudly give it to me. I'm delighted."

With the breathless excitement of an enthusiast, six-year-old Ava adds, "It's really fun to decoupage because I get all messy. There's a special watery glue and thin paintbrush. I pick out magazine pictures and a little brown box and then I cut them out and paste them on. Mom helped me a little because she told me to put the glue all over, but she isn't bossy. I get to do it by myself because it's my very own project. I can even clean up."

everlasting wreath

I f your mother is a saver like mine, perhaps this project will appeal to both of you. 🕯️🕯️🕯️ One day while we visited at her house, my mother asked me to help her clean out some of the drawers of accumulation that inevitably build up over time. One large drawer held several things that had sentimental value for one reason or another. Rocks and shells from our beach vacations, a damaged but still pretty beaded purse that her own mother once kept coins in, an inexpensive charm bracelet that I had given her one Christmas when I was eleven, souvenir spoons from a collection now scattered, and a few small pieces of china. My mother put them all into a box and asked me to take them home. "You'll think of something to do with them," she said with a smile. 🕯️🕯️🕯️ The assortment of things looked as though they belonged together. The colors and sizes connected visually and emotionally.

CHANCE FAVORS THE PREPARED MIND.

— LOUIS PASTEUR —

Remembering the empty grapevine wreath hanging on the garage wall, I decided to suggest the future project then and there—to decorate the wreath with this ragtag collection as a kind of 3-D scrapbook. A quick trip to town for a bunch of greens from the flower shop and we were all set. 🌿🌿🌿 Using a paddle of wire, we covered the bare wreath with sprigs of lemon leaf and eucalyptus. Then we arranged the odds and ends here and there still using the wire to fasten them into place. Suddenly, the box was empty, the wreath complete. It was a delightful way to spend an afternoon together, reminiscing about each piece of memorabilia and working side by side. Best of all, I didn't take all those things back to my house. My mother loved our wreath creation and happily kept it—proudly hanging it in the living room.

you will need

TO MAKE A WREATH:
- A WREATH FORM SUCH AS GRAPEVINE, STRAW, OR RATTAN
- 12 SPRAYS OF LEMON LEAF (FLORIST SHOPS USE THESE AS FILLER IN ARRANGEMENTS)
- GERMAN STATICE, BABY'S BREATH, OR SEEDED EUCALYPTUS
- 9 TO 12 DRIED ROSES
- A COLLECTION OF OBJECTS WITH A NEUTRAL COLOR THEME

TOOLS:
- A PADDLE OF FLORAL WIRE AND WIRE CUTTERS

BEGIN BY COVERING the wreath with the lemon leaf. Lay it onto the form and use the paddle of wire to wrap around the wreath and leaves. Continue to cover each wrap with another bunch of leaves, each time hiding the wire wrap on the previous branch. It's easier than it sounds; the big leaves cover easily. Occasionally add another floral accent like the sprigs of statice or eucalyptus. When the wreath is fully covered, choose a top and wire a hanger to the back.

LAY THE WREATH flat again and arrange clusters of decorations. Shells and rocks, silver spoons, and china can be securely wrapped with wire without attempting to conceal the wire. In fact, it adds to the charm. Remove the dried roses from their stems and run a wire strand through the base of one. Repeat this with other buds until one strand of wire holds several flowers. Close the wire strand to form a tight, braceletlike cluster of buds that can be wired in one piece to the wreath. Wire the remaining decorations into place according to kind and color. Allow some decorations to hang into the interior of the wreath or stand an antique postcard there.

cookie candle box

This is our idea of a perfect gingerbread house: fabulous and easy. The daunting task of making a whole gingerbread house would keep us from the project, but this one is just right for a wintery afternoon in February—or any other time, for that matter. ✖✖✖ Like a set on a Hollywood movie lot, it is really just a house facade with sides only big enough to hold it upright. But sitting on the mantel with a candle behind it, the glow at dusk is truly enchanting. ✖✖✖ We have made several architectural versions over the years modeled after a friend's original holiday gift, always marveling at the simplicity and at the delight it provides with very little time and trouble. ✖✖✖ Let your daughter design the house—perhaps to resemble your own, a relative's, or a friend's house facade.

THERE ARE TWO WAYS OF SPREADING LIGHT: TO BE THE CANDLE
OR THE MIRROR THAT REFLECTS IT.

— EDITH WHARTON —

you will need

TO MAKE ONE CANDLE HOUSE:

A RECIPE FOR GINGERBREAD COOKIES:

- 1/2 CUP BUTTER
- 1/4 CUP SUGAR
- 1/4 CUP PACKED BROWN SUGAR
- 1 EGG
- 1/2 CUP MOLASSES
- 3 CUPS FLOUR
- 1/2 TSP. EACH SALT, CINNAMON, GINGER, NUTMEG, CLOVES

A RECIPE FOR ROYAL ICING:

- 2 EGG WHITES (ROOM TEMPERATURE)
- 1/4 TSP. CREAM OF TARTAR
- 3 CUPS POWDERED SUGAR

- A CARDBOARD BASE APPROXIMATELY 8″ x 6″
- A VOTIVE CANDLE
- SILVER DRAGEES OR RED HOT CANDIES

TOOLS:

- PARCHMENT PAPER, BAKING SHEET, ROLLING PIN, A SHARP KNIFE, A PASTRY BAG WITH TIP

------

*If a project is
too complicated, simplify it
by making some of it
ahead of time.
Cut, glue, or mix portions
in advance.*

✖✖ ENLARGE AND TRANSFER pattern from page 156 or draw your own design onto parchment paper. Cut out the silhouette of the building shape but not the window details, and set aside. Cover the cardboard base with a piece of foil, taping securely underneath. Set aside. To mix the cookie dough, cream the butter with the sugars. Add the egg, then the molasses. Add the flour with spices to make a stiff dough. Chill in plastic wrap for an hour. On a cookie sheet, roll the dough out to a rectangle that will fit your house silhouette. It should be about 1/4″ thick. Spray the parchment paper template with cooking spray and then dust with flour to prevent it from sticking to the cookie dough. Place it onto the rolled dough. With a sharp knife, cut out the general shape of the house, adding a 1/8″ rim on all edges. If you wish, cut out decorative edges at the roofline. Remove the paper and cut out a door and windows here and there. Be careful not to compromise the overall strength of the cookie by cutting too much. Reserve the window and door cutouts and split each lengthwise. Dip your finger in water and paint the back of the cutouts to add as shutters to the window openings if you like, or reserve and add them later with icing.

✸✸ **FROM THE REMAINING DOUGH**, cut out two wall sides 4″ × 5″, cutting one top diagonally to the right and the other to the left. Cut a freehand or cookie cutter heart out of each side and add as you did the shutters in any spot you like. Bake the completed cookies at 325° for twenty minutes. Be careful not to overbake. Allow to cool one minute, then gently loosen cookies from sheet. Cool ten more minutes, then remove to a wire rack to finish cooling completely.

✸✸ **MIX ROYAL ICING** by beating egg whites and cream of tartar in a large mixing bowl. When foamy, add sugar gradually and continue beating for five to seven minutes, until stiff. Cover with plastic wrap. Fill the pastry bag (fitted with a plain tip) with icing and pipe a line along the edge of the

unfloured side of the parchment paper house template. Place the cookie front on the template so that the template attaches to the back of the cookie. This makes the frosty window panes.

✸✸ **DECORATE THE HOUSE FRONT** and sides as you wish. Add silver dragees or red hots for accents. Allow to dry for an hour. On the cardboard base, pipe a generously thick U-shaped line of icing across the front and sides an inch away from the edge to match the dimensions of the house front and sides. Think of a snowbank. Pipe a thick line on the taller edges of the corresponding wall sides that will attach to the house front. Set the front of the house into the icing, adjusting it and holding it upright with one hand. Add the side walls and butt them against the front so that the icing cements them. Hold for several minutes while the icing joints set. Allow to dry undisturbed for several hours.

✸✸ **WE LATER ADDED** a parchment paper scallop fence around the front to disguise less-than-perfect icing and a pair of bottle brush trees anchored with a dab of icing. Place a glass votive candle in a glass holder inside and light the candle. Place on a mantel, deep windowsill, or sideboard out of the reach of curious children. Never leave a candle unattended.

TEDDY BEAR AND RABBIT

PAGE

72

DECORATED SUITCASE

PAGE

76

KITTY CAT PILLOW

PAGE

78

all day

The chance to spend an entire day together is one that warrants some thought and planning. If you didn't have a daughter and a friend called you to ask if you would entertain her daughter for a whole day, wouldn't you plan all kinds of things to fill the time? ✧✧✧ And wouldn't they be fun for you, too? Our own daughters and mothers deserve the same special treatment. So given a day for just the two or three of you, be prepared with a short list of ideas and a basket of supplies to make something together.

WHAT YOU WILL DO MATTERS.

ALL YOU NEED IS TO DO IT.

— JUDY GRAHN —

WALL POCKET

PAGE

82

DOLL ARMOIRE

PAGE

86

PATCHWORK THROW

PAGE

90

SOPA DE LIMA

PAGE 94

The same advice extends to a visit with a grandmother or a doting aunt who would love the idea of a project. This isn't to say you should be huddled around a worktable all day, but an easy project suited to your interests and skills allows you to be together in a productive way.

One summer, several friends and I designed a co-op enrichment program for five busy but determined mothers and eight starry-eyed children. Each mother took a day of the week and led an activity for the group based on her own special area of expertise. Nan, the costume collector, directed a series of skits and a costume show. Pat, the display designer, helped them to craft life-size self-portraits, and Lee, a renowned cook and caterer, taught them to bake bread. Robyn, an editor, took them to the city for cultural tours, and I painted secondhand furniture with them in the backyard. The children, now in college, still refer to that magical few weeks as the best summer camp ever. The mothers delight

in the same sentiments and wish we could do it all again.

Make the most of your talents and desires—and share them with your loved ones. These small endeavors furnish the mind and heart with the cherished memories we will someday hold dearest.

teddy bear & rabbit

The first time I made this bear was on a rainy vacation in the north woods of Wisconsin in the middle of nowhere. Other than the dime store, there weren't many options in town for project supplies. ❧ ❧ ❧ Luckily, there was a thrift shop. We bought an old woolly butterscotch sweater and headed for the Laundromat, where we needed to wash wet jeans and sweatshirts anyway. Felted in the washer and dryer, the sweater was so soft we knew it wanted to be recast as a bear. We drew some pattern shapes out of newspaper, and soon enough, he came to life. ❧ ❧ ❧ Corny as it sounds, the personality of a doll or animal presents itself as soon as the face is stitched on—the placement of eyes, nose, and mouth—even ears—determines an expression that makes it instantly unique. It really is like meeting a new friend with a personality all his own.

A HOMEMADE FRIEND WEARS LONGER THAN ONE
YOU BUY IN THE MARKET.

— AUSTIN O'MALLEY —

This wide-eyed bear has been the darling of our house, perhaps because he has such a quizzical, begging look about him. Although he was originally pronounced a boy, he had to become a she-bear once his wardrobe began to include skirts and dresses.

✿ WASH AND DRY the sweater to felt it. Enlarge and transfer the pattern pieces from page 156 to tracing paper. (To make a rabbit, use the same pattern and method, but make the ears taller and add a tail. The tail is just a circle of wool pinched and gathered up in the middle with a few stitches and then sewn to the back.) Cut out the shapes and pin to the fabric, being careful to have the grain going vertically. Cut out the pieces and begin stitching the head with a whipstitch on the raw edges. With the right side out, sew one head side to one side of the head top

you will need

- A WOOL SWEATER OR A LENGTH OF FLANNEL WOOL OR PLUSH FELT
- WHITE FELT FOR EYES, BLACK FOR NOSE
- BLACK EMBROIDERY THREAD OR PEARL COTTON
- POLYESTER STUFFING
- UNCOOKED RICE
TOOLS:
- TRACING PAPER, PENCIL, SCISSORS, NEEDLE AND PINS, SEWING THREAD TO MATCH THE SWEATER COLOR

and then match the other head side to the other top edge and stitch in place. Stitch the two head sides together along the bottom from the nose to the bottom of the neck. Pin the head back to the triangular face edges. I like to loosely stuff the face at this point so that I can get the back on and shape it as I like it, tucking in the ears where they seem to go best.

✿ THE EARS SHOULD be pinched a bit at the bottoms before they are tucked into the seam as this makes them curl forward with a bit more character. If they look too large and mousey, they can be trimmed a bit or pushed farther down into the head. Stitch all around the back of the head, including through the ears. The head will be completely finished then, like a ball with ears.

✿ TO MAKE A FACE, use black pearl cotton or black embroidery thread. After pinning the eye rounds into place as you like them, keep the knot at the neck bottom and stitch the eyes into place by centering a French knot in the center of the white wool eye. Using the same black thread, stitch the nose piece into place and add two stitches for a mouth. Knot the thread at the neck bottom. Set the head aside.

✿ STITCH THE DARTS on the body front and the body back, which will make it easier for the bear to bend and sit. If you prefer a standing bear, you can skip this step. Wrong sides together, whipstitch the front to the back, leaving the neck and feet open at the bottoms. Stitch the feet rounds into the openings. Fill the feet with a few tablespoons of uncooked rice and then loosely stuff the body with polyester stuffing. For a bendable bear, do not overstuff the body. Stitch the head to the body securely all around the neck twice with a blindstitch.

hand sewing
How many times I have admired a hand-sewn garment, handkerchief, or framed needlework and wished that I could sit beside the needleworker to learn her secrets of sewing. Perhaps because I sat beside my own mother, watching her smock, mend, and needlepoint, I have a great appreciation for the power of the needle.

Though sewing was a necessary skill in order to have clothing, through the years it has become something well beyond that.

WHETHER THE DECORATIVE stitchery adorns a moccasin or a piece of table linen, the patterns tell an intricate story of women and their craftsmanship—a story rich with images from a cultural legend told in pictures, a heritage and homeland left across the sea, a young lesson in life, a sentimental scene glimpsed daily at the window, or a dreamy fantasy only imagined. Even the embroidered buttonhole on a dress speaks of necessity and personal adornment combined with great affection.

Almost every culture has some form of embroidery to call its own, traditionally a legacy to pass from mother to child. Through the generations, family styles and expertise developed in a household where a mother and daughter worked with the materials most readily available to their region and means. Native plant dyes or imported silk thread, barnyard feed sacks or linen canvas from Europe, the materials affected the look and the design of the finished work. As in other crafts, American needleworkers are known for their true resourcefulness and independence. A sturdy scrap of cloth cut away from a deteriorating garment could be embellished with embroidery to become part of a quilt, a table runner, or a sampler. Every young girl was expected to take up the needle and master enough stitches to carry on the tradition and to practice patience. Her mother taught this along with other necessary household pursuits.

Sewing, however, eventually became a leisure craft to be enjoyed at day's end when a rare moment of relaxation presented itself. As women's lives became simpler and more materials from abroad became available, this opportunity increased. Crewel work and needlepoint are still enjoyed by women today, but the most popular embroidery form is the cross-stitch. There are even computer programs now that will adapt designs to cross-stitch grids. The simplicity of technique and materials makes this a craft for mother and daughter to explore quite easily. A hoop, a needle, floss, fabric, and an idea are all that is needed to start. Even a kitchen dish towel will look prettier with a bit of stitchery at the edge. It doesn't take long to develop a style and ease with the needle that will make this a favorite pastime.

decorated suitcase

Old vinyl suitcases from the sec-ondhand store are great to fool around with, especially if they come cheap. I buy several at a time and keep them stashed in a closet. When the right time presents itself, I pull one out and transform it with paint (which sticks nicely to the vinyl texture) or paper cutouts. They are great for doll clothes, overnights, or makeup.

We have also made them for birthday, graduation, and bridal shower gifts. This kind of project is per-fect for a day home sick from school. Cutting out images from magazines or catalogs is easy to do in bed or on the couch, and then put away for a while. At our house, there have been some miraculous recoveries by inspired patients whose symptoms have suddenly disappeared in the face of a good time spent cutting and pasting with Mom.

you will need

TO MAKE ONE SUITCASE:
- AN OLD SUITCASE IN FAIR CONDITION
- MAGAZINES AND CATALOGS TO SNIP FROM

TOOLS:
- ACRYLIC PAINTS, SEALER, AND BRUSHES; SCISSORS AND DECOUPAGE MEDIUM

✦ **WASH THE SUITCASE** surface with a minimum of detergent water. Once the grime is gone and the suitcase is dry, paint it with a base coat color. Avoid painting metal handles and hinges. Arrange cutouts as you wish and then paint the backs with decoupage medium. Apply them like stickers, smoothing out the bubbles and edges. For painted designs, choose a simple overall pat-tern like big flowers or stripes. Randomly paint shapes on all sides, then go back and add details or filler leaves, insects, or dots. Use the same edge of the paintbrush to get uniform lines when needed When finished, seal applied cutouts and paint with an acrylic sealer for a finished look.

kitty cat pillow

Made from felted sweaters, one soft, striped crew neck inspired the cat and makes a strong focal point. Bits and pieces from the scrap bag were used to build a wreath of flowers and vines around the cat. Experiment with the colors available to you—though sometimes it is fun to hunt down the particular color that would make it all just right. ✖✖✖ Many of the tasks in this pillow are easily managed by a six-year-old. The drawing and cutting of pattern shapes will be improved by a child's imaginative hand. Perhaps she would like to draw your family pet or another from imagination. ✖✖✖ The folk art feel of the piece comes largely from her contribution to this design-and-cutting stage. Save the harder stitching later for yourself. Be flexible and make it your own with personal choices along the way.

NOTHING MAKES A HOUSE COZIER THAN CATS.

— GLADYS TABER —

you will need

TO MAKE ONE KITTY CAT PILLOW:

- A GREEN SWEATER SQUARE 16″ x 16″ FOR THE BACKGROUND
- A STRIPED SWEATER OR OTHER PATTERN FOR THE CAT
- 10″ PIECES OF YELLOW, YELLOW-GREEN, BLUE-GREEN, BLUE, INDIGO, LAVENDER, AND CRANBERRY FROM WOOL SWEATERS OR FABRIC SCRAPS
- WOOL YARN OR FLOSS IN COLORS TO MATCH YOUR SCRAPS
- FABRIC FOR THE PILLOW BACKING 16″ x 16″
- POLYESTER STUFFING

TOOLS:

- TRACING PAPER, SCISSORS, PAPER FOR TEMPLATES, PINS, AND A SEWING NEEDLE

BEGIN BY ENLARGING and tracing the pattern pieces from page 157 and transferring them to heavy paper to use as templates. Pin and cut out all the pieces from your prefelted sweaters, taking advantage of neckbands and other small scraps for vines and leaves. Pin each shape to the background, overlapping edges where necessary. Use yarn in matching colors (or contrast them for color richness—I used purple yarn for the blue flowers to give the blue more of a lavender look), and blanket stitch the pieces into place. Add details after the main design is stitched onto the background, but be sure to hide the knots on the back.

WHEN FINISHED, assemble the pillow with right sides facing and stitch around the edges, leaving an opening. Then turn right side out, stuff (your young daughter will love this part), and neatly stitch the opening closed.

creating a family portrait pillow

SIFT THROUGH THE FELT SCRAP basket and select several colors to use in a family portrait pillow. These paperdoll style people are somewhat primitive, but are enlivened by colorful fabrics and little details sewn on later with French knots or satin stitches. All the shapes we used were basically triangles (dresses), rectangles (pant legs and shirts) and little ovals for faces. Like Colorforms, we cut out freehand (though you could easily make paper patterns to try out first) and stacked the precut shapes into little stick figures. Blanket-stitched to a background, our fabric family portrait went off to college with Erin to keep her company.

wall pocket

There is nothing like the thrill of making something from resources that are already within reach inside a cupboard or the recycling bin. That might be why we make so many things out of papier-mâché. White glue, newspaper, flour, and cardboard are usually close at hand, and these simple materials contain many fabulous possibilities. ◉◉◉ Once the structure is assembled, the layering requires little or no concentration, so there's lots of time to talk and visit. ◉◉◉ This is a great project to make with a daughter who is home from college and who will appreciate this useful little wall pocket for her dorm room or apartment. Her design ideas are bound to be unexplored territory for you, and she will love to show you the newest trend. By all means, take notes and then make one of these for yourself, too.

SOME PURSUE HAPPINESS—OTHERS CREATE IT.

— ANONYMOUS —

you will need

TO MAKE A WALL POCKET WITH
  A MIRROR:
• A PIECE OF CARDBOARD
  APPROXIMATELY 18″ x 14″
• A MIRROR APPROXIMATELY
  4″ SQUARE
• PASTE FROM FLOUR, GLUE,
  AND WATER
• NEWSPAPER STRIPS
TOOLS:
• ACRYLIC PAINTS, BRUSHES,
  A BOX CUTTER OR CRAFT KNIFE,
  AND MASKING TAPE
• 8″ OF WIRE
• SANDPAPER

◎◎ ENLARGE AND TRACE the pattern from page 157, cut it out, and use it as a template for the cardboard piece. Trace around the template onto the cardboard and cut out the cardboard. Fold the pocket and its tabs along the marked lines and tape the pocket securely into place at the sides. Make a small pair of holes in the center of the back where the mirror will cover them later and fish a short length of wire through the holes. Twist on the mirror side of the back for a hanger. Cover the twist with masking tape.

◎◎ IN A SMALL BOWL, mix 1 cup warm water, 1/2 cup flour, and 1 tablespoon white glue to make the paste. Tear newspaper into 1″ wide strips to a length you like and dip them into the paste piece by piece. Apply each to the cardboard form in all directions and covering all areas (and the back, too). Be careful not to cover the hanger or to make the pocket too thick in any one place. Give special attention to the pocket area while layering the strips.

◎◎ LET THE FIRST LAYER dry and apply a second. To speed up the drying time, place it in a warm oven for about two hours (otherwise, you'll need to leave it overnight). Don't leave it in the direct sunlight, because it might warp. If it does warp, try weighting the edges with canned goods. When it is dry, sand the edges and base paint front and back with white acrylic paint.

◎◎ LATER YOU CAN GIVE it another color for a base coat and then glue the mirror into place. Paint on the designs of your choice or decoupage it with cutouts or colored tissue paper. When finished, seal it with a coat or two of acrylic sealer.

--- TOOL TOTE ---

For a different version, make a tool tote out of a tissue box. Cut the top off the box and make a partition with a handle out of cardboard. Cut the edges into an interesting design that will inspire paint designs after you papier-mâché the whole structure.

▼ ▼ ▼

pat and leah

Pat has always delighted in her daughter Leah's artistic endeavors, and she continues to be impressed by Leah's amazing creative output. "Even now at twenty years old, Leah is still filling our house with her latest projects. A young pal of hers once called our apartment 'Leah-land.' From the time when she was very little, she was constantly making things. Over the years she has experimented in-depth with ceramics, drawing, painting, papier-mâché, collage, photography, pop-up books, knitting, quilting, pattern making, and sewing."

BLESSED INFLUENCE OF ONE TRUE LOVING HUMAN SOUL ON ANOTHER!

GEORGE ELIOT

ALTHOUGH SOME OF THESE project experiments were new ground for Pat, she does have a keen eye for creative excellence and strong graphic design. She has chosen other works of art in the house in part to inspire her child's artistic sensibility. Pat would also bring home good books on design and crafts that she left in Leah's way so that she could flip through them. If Leah wanted to try something, Pat would help her brainstorm the how-to, gather all the materials needed, and then look for ways to be the assistant. "I didn't push it, though. Mostly, I just wanted to get her started. She always did the rest herself. Once I brought home a flyer about an art show in town that I thought she might like to go to. She didn't want to go; she wanted to be in it! Sure enough, she and her friend Julia got into anything they could make with papier-mâché. Every day after school they worked on their wares with determination. Boxes, vases, picture frames, wands, puppets. It was remarkable what they made. Their booth sold out quickly, and now I wish I'd bought the whole collection."

Appreciation for a child's efforts is essential. "I think it is important to display everything your children create—to make your approval visible and to indicate that you always have room for more. Once I went into a local frame shop with some of Leah's drawings. There were a lot of them; of course, I wanted to frame them all. The man at the shop said, 'Boy, you sure are nice to your daughter.' He seemed to be incredulous that I would spend real money to frame my child's art. I guess he missed the point. I was framing these drawings so that I could hang them up for all the world to see and inspire her to create more. It worked! I took her art seriously and so does Leah."

doll armoire

Knowing that a well-stocked materials closet is essential for spontaneous projects, I purchased an unpainted doll armoire from the craft store and tucked it away. Small cupboards are somehow irresistible, and a place for doll clothes seemed like a good idea for Maury, who still loves her dolls. ❧ ❧ ❧ Soon enough came a summer day without an agenda and an idle ten-year-old in my midst. The suggestion of dolls was instantly dismissed as ridiculous —overnight that notion had suddenly become far too childish to serve as a means of entertainment. But I can tell you that once the cupboard was all painted up especially for them, the dolls overran the living room for several days. ❧ ❧ ❧ Planning, priming, experimenting, correcting, and collaborating filled the day with a mission to transform the plain-Jane cupboard into a masterpiece.

LUCK IS A MATTER OF PREPARATION MEETING OPPORTUNITY.

— OPRAH WINFREY —

aury learned how to apply a checkerboard pattern with a sponge square, how to paint a flower in a repeat pattern, and how to tell her mom in a nice way that she didn't care for some of my tinkering with her work. "How did that flower get those spots on it?" she wondered. She liked it better before I "enhanced" it. Point taken. I painted out the spots.

you will need

TO MAKE ONE DOLL ARMOIRE:
- AN UNPAINTED ARMOIRE FROM THE CRAFT STORE
- WHITE PRIMER PAINT
- ACRYLIC SEALER
TOOLS:
- SANDPAPER, COLORED ACRYLIC CRAFT PAINTS, BRUSHES IN A VARIETY OF SIZES, A DRY KITCHEN SPONGE

BEGIN BY SANDING any rough surfaces and edges. Wipe away the dust. Prime the cupboard inside and out with the white primer. Allow to dry for approximately two hours. Apply the base coat of paint in the manner you prefer— a light coat with the primer showing through or a strong coat of color. You might need a second coat to achieve this.

EXPERIMENT WITH DECORATIVE treatments such as an overall checkerboard pattern created from a piece of the kitchen sponge. To do this, cut a strip of sponge so that each end is a square stamp. Dip the stamp in a pool of paint and bounce it on newspaper to remove the excess paint. Then stamp the side panels of the armoire with the stamp in a horizontal row, skipping a space each time, refilling with paint as necessary. On the next row, stamp below the unstamped spaces to make the checkered pattern. Look ahead now and then to keep your lines straight. The irregularity of the technique is appealing and will forgive mistakes or crooked lines. Overall, the eye will not detect the unevenness as much as you think.

THE SAME IDEA is used for the stripes at the door edges. A wide brush filled with paint will leave striped strokes if applied steadily and quickly. It takes a bit of practice, which can be done on newspaper first. The inset panels of the doors were marked off into diamonds to create smaller areas for decoration. Maury painted a simple flower on one diamond, a second on another. She repeated these two flower designs on the remaining diamonds with the same paint schemes. A few more simple brush strokes, dots, dashes, and loops placed in a methodical way create the remaining details. Ribbony vines added to the side panels and dots splashed onto the lower trim continue the layering of simple pattern and texture that makes a piece like this interesting. Staying with a limited color palette makes it all work together. The insides of the doors offer more decorative options. It's all up to you in terms of how much you want to do.

FINISH YOUR WORK with a coat or two of acrylic sealer. Encourage her to sign her initials and the date for future generations. This armoire is now most certainly an heirloom.

patchwork throw

Although this project could be made with hand-knitted squares, our version takes a big shortcut and uses felted squares from old sweaters. The same sweaters that supplied the material for the tea cozy and the kitty pillow, in fact, easily left enough for this patch throw. ✖✖✖ This one is perfect for a baby blanket, but could be made larger with more squares for a lap blanket or even a bed-size one. You might want to consider adding felt decorations to the squares such as the simple flowers used in other projects. ✖✖✖ The possibilities for design and pattern are really endless, depending on the sweaters. The striped sweater that we have loved so much for its color and pattern adds a nice graphic touch to otherwise gentle shades of green, lavender, and blue.

DIAMONDS ARE ONLY CHUNKS OF COAL THAT STUCK
TO THEIR JOBS, YOU SEE.

— MINNIE RICHARD SMITH —

XX AFTER FELTING A SELECTION of sweaters in the washer and dryer, cut the sweaters into panels of usable fabric. Make a template for a 4 1/2" square from cardboard and cut squares from the sweaters to this size, being careful to stay with the grain of the knit. You will need forty-eight squares (another chance to review math concepts with a young daughter) in the combination of colors you prefer. Lay them out on a table and arrange a design that you like. It is interesting to mix right sides and wrong sides and to vary the texture and grain of the different knits.

XX BEGIN WITH THE BOTTOM left pair and, using a zigzag stitch set to its widest capacity, butt the two squares together (without overlapping) beneath the presser foot and stitch right down the center of the butted edges. A beginning sewer can do this with a little practice on a scrap first. The puckering created by the stitching becomes part of the design. Continue to add squares in the pattern you have created to complete one row. Then make another row and add the second row to the first in the same manner, pinning the rows first to match seams.

XX WHEN THE BLANKET is fully assembled, zigzag around the outside edge to finish. The puckered ruffle will mimic the other seams and makes a lovely, easy finish. If there is fabric remaining, this method makes an excellent and fast doll blanket.

you will need

TO MAKE A BLANKET MEASURING
26" x 36":
• GRASSY GREEN, GRAY, LIGHT BLUE,
  TURQUOISE, LAVENDER, INDIGO,
  GRAY-STRIPED SWEATERS
TOOLS:
• SEWING MACHINE WITH A ZIGZAG
  STITCH, THREAD, SCISSORS,
  RULER, TEMPLATE

- - - - - -

*Ziploc plastic bags are handy for keeping
small projects together.*

*Find an old vintage craft magazine and
see how you might update the work
with materials available now.*

- - - - - -

jill, chelseah, lauren, and erica

After moving to California, Jill and her three daughters became involved in community service through the National Charity League. A mother-daughter organization that serves various philanthropies in the area, the league encourages its volunteers to work together to create various craft projects for the different charities. "The crafts are fun to do together and an opportunity to pass on many skills that are lost or forgotten today."

"FROM TERRY-CLOTH pet beds for the Humane Society, flannel baby blankets for the hospital, hand-painted ornaments to decorate Christmas trees for the wards. There are lots of ways to reach out to those in need of comfort. However, our family's specialty is the six-inch knitted square." Jill fishes one out of a basket on the kitchen counter and holds it up. Perhaps not quite square, it looks a bit like a potholder. She explains that it is just one of many that they have knitted this year. The basket full of squares will be sent to the Red Cross, where they are sewn together to make lap blankets

"Knitting is a craft my mom taught me when I was just twelve. Mom was making a bright orange sweater when I asked her if she would show me how to knit. Consequently, my first knitted project was a bright orange bookmark. She must have had a lot of orange yarn, because my second project was an orange muffler. I don't remember anyone in the family ever wearing her finished sweater. Maybe it was because I used so much of the yarn in my muffler. The real project, though, wasn't so much the finished work. It was more the one-on-one time with Mom.

"Today we don't have as much down time as when I was growing up. But I taught my daughters, Chelseah, Lauren, and Erica, to knit on a cross-country road trip when we were held captive in the car for hours on end. It took a while to get the gauge right, but once they got the hang of it, they really seemed to enjoy knitting. Our first 'knitting trip' was from Los Angeles to Park City, Utah. We knitted over ten squares. The great thing about knitting—this project especially—is that without having to concentrate on a pattern, we could enjoy the scenery and each others company, too. That was our navy blue and forest green trip. Erica chose the colors for our last trip, lemon yellow and lavender.

"I love to knit, and I am happy to pass that legacy on to my girls. I know in our future we may take on something bigger than our six-inch squares, but if nothing else, I hope those squares hold the same shared memories for my girls as they do for me. We can only imagine the Red Cross lap blankets that we have helped make, but the reward is in knowing our squares have made a blanket special for someone. It has been quite special for us, too."

sopa de lima

Homemade soup is one of the great pleasures in life—to make, to serve, and to eat. This particular soup is especially enjoyable because it has a variety of textures that please children. Crushing tortilla chips, squeezing lime wedges, and sprinkling with grated cheese are the final flourishes to a very hearty dish popular in Mexico.

◉◉ **WASH AND DRY** the chicken. Place it in a six-quart kettle and add water to cover the chicken. Add the chopped onion, salt, and pepper. Simmer for two hours or so, until the chicken begins to come off the bones. Remove from heat and lift chicken with a slotted spoon, placing it into a bowl to cool. Cool broth and remove fat accumulation from the top. Add the canned tomatoes, crushing by hand as you add them. Simmer broth gently. Remove skin and bones from chicken and return shredded chicken pieces to the simmering broth. Add chopped cilantro and cook for thirty minutes.

◉◉ **LADLE INTO LARGE** soup bowls and serve with a basket of crisp tortilla chips, grated cheddar or jack cheese, and wedges of fresh lime. Garnish with some of each.

you will need

TO MAKE SOUP FOR EIGHT PEOPLE:
- ONE WHOLE CHICKEN (3 TO 4 POUNDS)
- WATER TO COVER (12 TO 14 CUPS)
- 1 LARGE SPANISH ONION, CHOPPED
- 1 TSP. SALT
- FRESH PEPPER TO TASTE
- 1 (28-OUNCE) CAN WHOLE TOMATOES
- ¼ CUP CHOPPED FRESH CILANTRO
- TORTILLA CHIPS
- CHEDDAR OR JACK CHEESE
- LIME WEDGES

MEMORY JAR AND LAMP

PAGE

98

PATCHWORK PILLOW

PAGE

102

TABLE RUNNER AND NAPKINS

PAGE

106

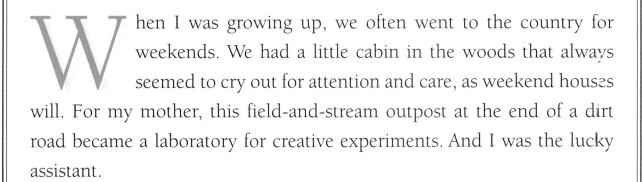

over the weekend

W hen I was growing up, we often went to the country for weekends. We had a little cabin in the woods that always seemed to cry out for attention and care, as weekend houses will. For my mother, this field-and-stream outpost at the end of a dirt road became a laboratory for creative experiments. And I was the lucky assistant.

THE MORE THE HEART IS NOURISHED WITH HAPPINESS,
THE MORE IT IS INSATIABLE.

— GABRIELLE ROY —

CROSS-STITCH SAMPLER

PAINTED RECIPE CHAIR

HOOKED FOOTSTOOL

EASEL CLOCK

PAGE 122

On Saturdays we usually went to local auctions and brought assorted treasures home to fool around with for the rest of the weekend. What fun we had transforming the finds, the cabin, and the weekend itself with our ingenuity. Relying on simple materials available out of a sewing box, paint cupboard, or pantry, we whipped up some true mother-daughter masterpieces. One day we painted all the kitchen chairs and discovered they were still sticky at dinnertime. Eating dinner on our laps by the campfire that night was so much fun that it became a weekend tradition.

Several of the projects offered in this chapter are just the kind of thing we would have taken on to keep ourselves busy between hiking, reading, and baking. Taken one step at a time, the projects aren't especially demanding. You might consider moving the whole operation outside for a change of scenery or certainly to enjoy it so much that nothing else matters until it's complete. Few things compare to the pleasure of falling into a project so thoroughly that you lose track of time and all the business of everyday life. Suddenly you look up and it's dinnertime. Plan ahead just enough to have something in the house that you can cook quickly and maybe even eat on your laps if the chairs need a few more hours undisturbed.

memory jar & lamp

This project was so much fun that we were tempted to keep going and slather cement onto the kitchen table itself and cover it with the rest of the buttons, toys, trinkets, and alphabets that still remained on the collecting tray. I suppose that could actually be done and then one might place a glass top onto the collage. ◈◈◈ It would certainly make for interesting dinner table talk, but for starters, this pottery jug and the lamp base provided just the right amount of surface for a weekend project. ◈◈◈ Over the course of two days, I decorated the jug with Erin, whose eye for composition and restraint kept it from becoming too magnificently overdone, but the lamp was purely the creation of eleven-year-old Maury. In only two hours! She was simply unstoppable in her enthusiasm for sticking "stuff" into the cement.

LOVE IS A CANVAS FURNISHED BY NATURE AND
EMBROIDERED BY IMAGINATION.

— VOLTAIRE —

After cleaning out every junk drawer, basket bottom, shoe box, and doll case, she had an endless assortment of odds and ends to use, and she tried to pose each little trinket into the mix. I assisted by applying the cement to the lamp in sections ahead of her, but it seemed that she filled the sections faster than I could keep up.

I was quite impressed with her clever parade of toys standing straight up around the top; I would never have thought of that, and the overall effect made it look especially animated. The polar bear appears to be rolling a ball down the side over the lettered word *junk*. (No, I did not ruin the family board game. I was lucky enough to find a bag of letter tiles at a house sale.) With each project and each daughter, we had a chance to reminisce the past life of every solitary doll shoe, softball medal, and rubber frog.

Although it was a fast-moving ride, we headed down Memory Lane, stopping off for broken pieces of dress-up jewelry, keys to teen diaries, and left-over buttons from baby dresses made long ago. Rhinestone jewelry bits prompted discussions about Grammy's tea parties; Scout pins called up the names of old friends. I thought it remarkable to see that a tiny, scuffed hair barrette could summon the memory of an entire school year.

A few nights later at the amusement park, Maury turned in her hard-won prize coupons and selected a new sack full of plastic lizards and glittery gems. As we walked by all the long lines for rides that we hadn't had a chance to try yet, she inspected the sackful of prizes and asked, "Won't these look great in cement? Let's go home and make another lamp." My thoughts exactly. I couldn't have planned a sweeter escape.

you will need

TO MAKE ONE POT OR LAMP:
- A POTTERY JUG, VASE, OR POT ABOUT 12" TALL, OR A SMALL BEDROOM LAMP WITH A SHADE
- A TILE CEMENT AND GROUT PRODUCT—PREMIXED, IF POSSIBLE
- ASSORTED CHARMS, TRINKETS, TOYS, BEADS, BUTTONS, MARBLES

TOOLS:
- PUTTY KNIFE, COTTON SWABS, ACRYLIC PAINTS, AND BRUSH

◆ CONSIDER THE JUNK that you have collected and arrange it into sorts that make sense to you or to your daughter: groups such as gold shiny pieces, or goofy toys, or elegant buttons, or things that you love the most and want to feature prominently. When it's time to stick the trinkets into the cement, it's a good idea to have them in these pools on a tray to pick from quickly. The cement can be washed off before it dries if you make a

choice that must be changed, but it's best to have everything pretty handy and hope to avoid that.

◆ WE CHOSE TO BEGIN with the bottom of the back so that we would have the technique down pat by the time we hit the front center top. For that section we saved favorite things and even laid them out in a pattern on the table before planting them into the cement.

◆ USE THE PUTTY KNIFE to apply a thick 3/8" layer of cement to a small section (4" to 6" square) on the surface of the pot or lamp. Smooth it out somewhat with a plastic glove or a sandwich bag over your fingertip (use a patting motion) and feather the edges where the cement stops. Pose the ornaments into the cement piece by piece so that they are firmly planted but not pushed in so deeply that the cement oozes up and obscures the object. Use little beads or buttons to fill the in-between spots. This would be an excellent moment to involve a very young daughter who wants to pitch in as an assistant.

◆ USE THE COTTON SWABS, dampened when necessary, to clean off cement smudges or push the cement into place. Check often for stray cement that needs cleaning up. As you finish an area, apply more cement to the base, overlapping the feathered edge of the previous section, and continue the process until you have covered the whole base. This could be done one side at a time if you need to take a break. The cement air-dries on its own, but may take a few days. You might also want to lift the project onto an inverted clay pot so that the air can get under it and dry the bottom.

◆ TO IMPROVE THE LOOK of the lamp shade, we used a broad paintbrush and acrylic paint to stripe the shade vertically all around in one direction and then horizontally, too.

patchwork pillow

I like to sew by hand, always have. It's a peaceful, comforting activity that allows me to daydream or talk at the same time. ✧ ✧ ✧ Recently, I was at work on a small project rapidly filling a lazy, unstructured Sunday. It began to snow, and Maury came to sit by me. I stopped working and we watched the big flakes sift downward beyond the window. She wondered what I was making. "Nothing special, just a bit of patchwork." "What's it going to be?" she asked. Actually, I didn't know. It could be a part of a bigger patchwork, it could be a pillow, it could go right back into the basket. ✧ ✧ ✧ She sorted through my basket of fabrics there on the floor and handed up two bright greens. "Put these in somewhere. They look like they go. You could make little leaves with them." Suddenly, she gave me a quick hug and said, "I like it when you sew. It makes me feel cozy." Then she went outside to surf in the snow, but that moment was enough to inspire a project to share.

CONFIDENCE IS A PLANT OF SLOW GROWTH.

— ANNA LEONOWENS —

102

All the decisions I made about that bit of patchwork from that moment on, I shared with her.

Maury spent an occasional hour at my side sewing some of the shapes together, and unlike needle-workers of long ago who would not tolerate a daughter's imperfect stitches, I did not correct her work. Those little stitches are what I like best about it. I treasure them as they are, uneven and barely strong enough to hold together. This is a tangible memory of her vanishing girlhood, and whenever I look at these irregular, wandering threads, I will always see my little girl, heavily intent upon the effort of perfection, clenched lips, locked gaze, trying so hard to succeed in this small task without pricking herself on the needle or hopelessly tangling the thread. Watching her then and now, proud of her efforts, delighted to have sewn a simple seam, I know what she meant. For me, this is the definition of *cozy*.

you will need

TO MAKE A PATCHWORK PILLOW
18" x 12":
• ASSORTED SWEATERS OR FLEECE IN RED, TURQUOISE, BLUE, GREEN, LAVENDER, GRAY, ORANGE, YELLOW, WHITE
• BACKING FABRIC 19" x 13"
• PILLOW STUFFING
TOOLS:
• PAPER, PENCIL, SEWING THREAD, NEEDLE, SCISSORS, AND PINS

TRANSFER THE PATTERNS from page 158 to paper and cut out the shapes to use as templates. Feel free to make your own adjustments and change the patterns to reflect your own design ideas. Cut out the background squares of fabric from the felted sweaters or fleece, butting edges and sewing the blocks together to create a large patchwork rectangle. With white thread, baste a 1/2" border all around, which will serve as a seam allowance later, when you construct the pillow. Cut out the design shapes and pin them to the background patchwork. Use a hemstitch and regular sewing thread and needle to sew them into place. As with other projects sewn in this way, the stitches pretty much disappear into the plushness of the fabrics, so it is more important to make sure they are well attached rather than perfectly sewn. Place the finished work facedown on the right side of the backing fabric, cut to the same size. Machine or hand stitch along the white basting line, leaving an opening at the pillow bottom. Remove white basting, turn inside out, stuff, and blindstitch the opening shut.

anne and maggie

Anne sat down with her mother, sisters, cousins, and aunts at a family reunion. Together they opened a box filled with her grandmother's embroidered linens. Inside there was an incredible collection of cross-stitch patterns, free-hand design on pillowcases, hand towels, and table runners. You could almost see the years of her life measured in embroidery stitches. Everyone had a story to tell about Grandmother, and no one could remember Grandmother without a project held tightly in a hoop, threaded needle working stitches while she visited with family. She loved this craft.

THE MARK OF A
GOOD PARENT IS THAT
SHE CAN HAVE FUN
WHILE BEING ONE.

———

MARCELENE COX

ANNE'S DAUGHTER, Maggie, nine years old, swooped by to ask a question, but took an empty chair and joined the women inspecting every piece of handwork passed around the circle. She was fascinated by the colorful imagery, the careful stitches, and the connection to the past. Anne could see Maggie's curiosity rising and suspected that this was more than a passing interest.

Sure enough, on the car ride home Maggie didn't waste any time proposing an embroidery project of her own—a table runner for Thanksgiving in the tradition of her great-grandmother. For Anne there was a moment of panic when she realized that she knew very little about the craft. How would she help her daughter do this? Maggie had a clear idea of what the project should be, cross-stitched turkeys and border patterns of her own design. Anne is an illustrator and art director with lots of experience in home decorating, but sewing wasn't really her thing. "When we talked about how it would be made, I was thinking we would research turkeys and cross-stitch and make a pattern and then add it to a kit somehow. Maggie listened to my plan and then said that she would rather draw her own. Her plan was more like, 'Don't worry, Mom, we'll figure it out.' Fortunately, I realized I was making too much of it. So, instead, I focused on the fun we would have if I could relax and let her lead me. After all, it was her project. She didn't care if it was perfect; it was a first try and she loved inventing it along with her own style. That's what matters most. It's great that she has that courage to follow and trust her instincts. I'm so glad I caught on to what's really important here, because she just loved making that table runner. I gained new appreciation for my grandmother's craft and thought of her a lot while we sewed, sharing stories of my grandmother's wit and personality with Maggie. But mostly I enjoyed just being with her. I loved watching her careful hands, listening to her quick precise words as she instructed me on color and design, and her ease of praise for my own efforts. What can I say?—except that I adore her and I adore that table runner, too."

table runner & napkins

Decorations for the table are always a good choice for a project to do together. When the family sits down to share a meal, the evidence of your work is featured center stage. A young daughter will be so proud of her efforts and perhaps even recognize that this table runner set will be part of her home someday. This design takes advantage of simple materials and techniques similar to those used in vintage needlework projects from the 1930s. Large areas of the project were enhanced with painted shapes that give the project the appearance of more stitchery than was really used. Our colored prints were made from potato stamps and a simple stencil. Outlining the images with a running stitch adds visual strength and also offers an easy practice area for a quilting stitch to be used in later projects.

IT ISN'T THE GREAT BIG PLEASURES THAT COUNT THE MOST;
IT'S MAKING A GREAT DEAL OUT OF THE LITTLE ONES.

— JEAN WEBSTER —

The process could be varied to suit a number of seasonal colors and images. In fact, it didn't take us long to consider a spring design on white linen with pale pink dogwood petals and vines. This particular piece is especially pretty because the sophisticated colors evoke the style of the Arts and Crafts design period. Since you will need to buy enough fabric for a continuous length, napkins would be the best way to use the remaining panel while offering an excellent practice area for the stamping, painting, and stitching.

you will need

TO MAKE A RUNNER 20″ x 54″:
• 2 YARDS OF WASHABLE LINEN OR
  OTHER MEDIUM-WEIGHT FABRIC
• 3 OR 4 MEDIUM POTATOES
• A PIECE OF STENCIL PAPER 8″ x 10″
• FABRIC PAINTS IN GOLD,
  SAGE-GREEN, AND BROWN
• BLACK PEARL COTTON #5
TOOLS:
• MEASURING TAPE, SCISSORS,
  PENCIL, WATER-BASED MARKER,
  CRAFT KNIFE, FOAM BRUSH, AND
  EMBROIDERY NEEDLE

BEGIN BY WASHING and drying the fabric. Press while still slightly damp. Cut a runner 22″ x 56″ and use the measuring tape to mark the finished outline 1″ from the edge all around. With the marker, transfer each design image from page 157 to a potato cut in half lengthwise. Use the knife to outline the design (do this part yourself) and then cut away the potato around the design, leaving a depth of about 1/8″. Paint the stamp with a solid coat of fabric paint, being careful to not use too much paint. Stamp the image onto paper to test it.

THEN ALSO CUT OUT the rough shape from paper several times. Place the shapes where you plan to stamp the fabric and pin them into the design you are trying to achieve. This is especially important if you are after a symmetrical look.

PLACE A PAD of newspaper under the fabric where you will be stamping. Then remove each shape marker just before stamping and stamp there. Reposition the shapes as needed and pin again. If a young daughter is helping at this point, it's best not to try for a precise pattern. Something a little more random like an allover print will be more successful and considerably more fun. Keep in mind, too, that an uneven application of paint onto the stamp is bound to occur and will produce an uneven image. If this bothers you, use a cotton swab or a bristle brush barely wet with paint to fill in the unfilled spots. The unevenness, however, can be considered quite charming evidence of the handmade effort. When the paint is thoroughly dry in one area, continue in the next.

TO CREATE THE OVAL design in the middle of the runner, we placed a platter upside down on the runner and lightly penciled its outline. Then we stamped the leaves around it. When the stamping was complete, we cut a stencil (page

157) from a manila folder (you can also use stencil paper) and used a foam brush to fill in the stencil with gold paint. Later, when all paints have dried, heat-set the paint by ironing lightly from the back.

PLACE THE WORK in an embroidery hoop and use black pearl cotton to outline and connect the shapes with a simple running stitch. Use the same stitch to hem the edges. It's a lot simpler than it looks, and this easy stitch can be mastered by a beginning sewer in no time at all.

FOR THE NAPKINS, cut four squares, each approximately 16″ × 16″ or whatever size suits the remaining width of fabric. Stamp a design in one corner on each and outline and hem in the same manner as you did the runner.

cross-stitch sampler

We have a kitchen wall filled with framed samplers. The mottoes are sweet, simple, and inspirational, as are the scenes of little cottages with fences, pines, and flowers. Looking at them, I imagine the women who stitched these little pieces. Popular needlecraft kits in the 1940s and 1950s contained prestamped designs on linen cloth with skeins of floss. ✕✕✕ I have several examples of the same design made by different women, and the artistic differences clearly tell of true personalities I will never know. We redesigned a few of these to make our own and then transferred the diagram to leftover linen from the table runner. ✕✕✕ Cross-stitch is fairly easy, and frankly, the rough stitches of a child are more interesting to me than the near-perfect ones of an experienced adult.

THINGS TURN OUT BEST FOR PEOPLE WHO MAKE
THE BEST OF THE WAY THINGS TURN OUT.

— ANONYMOUS —

We were all pretty inexperienced with the needle here. Giving in to the imperfections of the work certainly added to the pleasure of an experimental project as well as to the lasting charm of our homemade first effort.

you will need

TO MAKE A MOTTO SAMPLER:

- A PIECE OF LINEN APPROXIMATELY 14″ X 18″
- EMBROIDERY FLOSS OR PEARL COTTON IN COLORS
- A FRAME WITH GLASS TO FIT

TOOLS:

- PENCIL, TRACING PAPER, TRANSFER PEN, SMALL EMBROIDERY HOOP, SHARP SCISSORS, AN EMBROIDERY NEEDLE, AN IRON

IF YOU WISH TO USE our design from page 158, enlarge it on a copier to the size of your pressed cloth. Place a sheet of tracing paper on it and trace the design. On the back of the traced image, go over the marks with a transfer pen. Place the tracing with transfer back transfer side down onto the straight weave of the fabric, positioning it carefully to stay centered. Pin into place and use an iron and manufacturer's directions from the transfer pen to heat-transfer the design onto the fabric.

PLACE THE CENTER of the work in the hoop. Cross-stitch begins in the lower-right corner of the stitch and goes diagonally upward and left to the next square. Continue through the row with these half stitches and return in the opposite direction to complete the bottom-left to upper-right halves of the stitches. Try to avoid knots on the back. It is preferable to stitch over an unknotted thread end and then to weave the thread end through the back of adjacent stitches. When finished, press again with the iron from the back. To frame, mount the work with double-sided tape onto an acid-free mat board backing cut to fit the interior of your frame.

Always be on the lookout for interesting picture frames. Those with gold leaf, old paint, or fine detailing will add character to your finished projects. Glass cut at the hardware store is inexpensive, and the finish work is very simple to do yourself.

painted recipe chair

I couldn't resist this chair at a house sale. Five dollars, already painted gold, sturdy, and good bones. Exactly the kind my mother would have dragged home from a country auction. It took me a while to get to it, but one rainy day, serendipity winked its eye in the direction of the lonesome basement chair. ❧ ❧ ❧ I really try to avoid the messy prep work that comes with repainting, so I opted for decoupage instead. What I love about this project, though, is the recipe hand-printed onto the chair seat like a giant recipe card. No need to flip through a cookbook; just stand up and there it is! It has always been my intention to make a set of these for a kitchen table when one of my daughters sets up house for the first time. That opportunity is yet to come, and this chair is still part of my dining room. We think the idea would also make a sweet shower gift for a bride or a rocker for an expectant mother with a lullaby or nursery rhyme instead.

MOST NEW DISCOVERIES ARE SUDDENLY SEEN THINGS
THAT WERE ALWAYS THERE.

— SUSANNE K. LANGER —

CLEAN UP THE CHAIR with mild soap and water. Apply a coat of antique gold spray paint, if desired, or work with the natural wood or paint color as is. If the existing finish has a lot of gloss on it, scuff it up with sandpaper wherever you plan to decoupage. Cut out a practice panel of newspaper to fit the chair seat (and back panel, if you have one suitable for decoration). Determine the placement of images on the flat surfaces of the chair and stick them on temporarily with teacher's putty to be sure you like the overall look when you stand back.

REMOVE THE NEWSPAPER panel for the seat, and use the marker to hand-print the recipe there. Try a decorative cut along the edges, if you like. It's a good idea to have a practice piece so that you can fit the recipe precisely onto the real one—save the financial pages with small print for the final copy. Ours took a few tries before we discovered the best placement of words and images.

WHEN YOU HAVE the recipe panel just the way you want it, paint the chair seat itself with decoupage medium and start at the back to roll the newsprint recipe onto the seat, smoothing out the wrinkles as you go. Don't fuss with the wrinkles too much because they will mostly disappear during the drying, but be sure that the air bubbles are pressed out.

WHEN DRY, ADD CUTOUTS where you want them on the recipe seat and elsewhere on the chair. We added more decoration with a small stencil and edged the chair seat with strokes from a small brush to make stripes. Then seal with two or three coats of acrylic sealer or decoupage medium.

you will need

TO DECORATE A CHAIR:

- A SECONDHAND CHAIR IN STURDY CONDITION
- ANTIQUE GOLD SPRAY PAINT, BLACK ACRYLIC PAINT
- CLIP ART IMAGES, PHOTOCOPIED
- NEWSPAPER AND PERMANENT MARKER
- A SMALL CHECKERED STENCIL
- 1/2" TO 1" WIDE BRUSH

TOOLS:

- SANDPAPER, POSTER PUTTY, DECOUPAGE MEDIUM, FOAM BRUSH, AND ACRYLIC SEALER

elizabeth and dora

"When I was in second grade, my best friend and I started an after-school craft club—just the two of us. We would take turns going to each other's house to make things. Her mom had all kinds of projects ready to go, jewelry, doll clothes, little paintings—something carefully planned out. My mom wasn't always as organized, but even when she was surprised by our sudden appearance, she was so happy to see us coming up the path after school, she would stop whatever she was busy with and quickly think of something we could do.

NOW I SEE THAT WITH five children, that was asking a lot. I'll always remember the fun we had being with her." Dora is in high school now and quite preoccupied with sports and schoolwork, but she knows that her mother, Elizabeth, still welcomes the occasional chance to drop everything for a moment together.

"Dora has watched me trying different hobbies and crafts over the years. I think she knows it's one way that women relax and share with each other, chatting while we work. At her age, it's important to have that chance to be together without having to really focus on one another. The work prompts conversations that lead in all directions, but it's the companionable silences that I love ... the moments when we are just there, side by side, content to be so."

Elizabeth has grown increasingly interested in rug hooking in recent years. She has attended classes and seminars on designing her own rugs and dying her own wool. On a trip to the rug supply shop with her mother, Dora picked a simple starter kit that her mother could help her begin. Elizabeth confides that she loves being the experienced pro in something she can share with Dora, a daughter talented and accomplished in all her efforts. Dora agreed that her mother is an exceptional teacher and says that she admires her creative departures from the rules of any project. "Mom trusts her own instincts about colors and design and then she does what she thinks will look best. Somehow it always does. As a beginner I find that comforting. I don't worry so much about mistakes."

Dora isn't quite sure that rug hooking will be her craft, but she's sticking with it a little longer. She admits that her mom might wind up finishing the design for her, but thinks that's okay. She echoes her mother's thoughts when she says that the memories of making the project together will be the heirloom she holds most dear.

SWEET IS THE SCENE WHERE
GENIAL FRIENDSHIP PLAYS
THE PLEASING GAME OF
INTERCHANGING PRAISE.

———

OLIVER WENDELL
HOLMES

hooked footstool

T his is one of those projects that developed quite spontaneously with great success. Maury was eight when she expressed an interest in learning to hook, so we took out a scrap of burlap and drew a flower on it. Hook in hand, she got the hang of it right away, and the flower started to spread out across the backing fairly quickly. ❧❧❧ Spying a scruffy little secondhand footstool nearby, she thought it would be possible to make a nice cover for the top. I steered her toward a design with a number of shapes and outlines that would allow her to change colors and fill the spaces easily. That way she could see quick progress, which is encouraging for a novice of any age. ❧❧❧ When finished, we tacked the hooked piece to the stool top as planned and hid the edges with a fancy tasseled trim. It has since become a permanent fixture in the living room, truly a favorite piece, and one to be admired for a great many reasons—rather like a home run first time at bat.

A JOURNEY OF A THOUSAND MILES MUST BEGIN WITH A SINGLE STEP.

— CHINESE PROVERB —

you will need

TO MAKE A FOOTSTOOL COVER
OR PILLOW:
• A FOOTSTOOL
• A PIECE OF RUG BURLAP OR MONK'S
  CLOTH LARGE ENOUGH TO STRETCH
  IN A RUG FRAME
• WOOL STRIPS CUT FROM FLANNEL
  WOOL YARDGOODS IN THE COLORS
  OF YOUR CHOICE OR 1/3 YARD
  60" GRAY-GREEN, 1/8 YARD MUSTARD-
  YELLOW, AND SCRAPS IN YELLOW,
  OATMEAL, KELLY GREEN, LEAF
  GREEN, DARK GREEN, RED, SALMON
• GIMP FRINGE AND GLUE TO ATTACH
TOOLS:
• A MARKER, MASKING TAPE, SCISSORS,
  A RUG HOOK, A RUG FRAME, THUMB-
  TACKS, PILLOW STUFFING OR QUILT
  BATTING, AND A STAPLE GUN

✷✷ ONCE YOU HAVE CUT the burlap to fit your frame, cover the raw edges with masking tape to keep them from unraveling. Draw the design from page 159 for the stool cover with marker on the front of the burlap, staying true to the weave of the background fabric. To make your own design, consider a paper cutting similar to the paper lace project in Chapter One. Unfold a simple cutting and trace around it for a template. Use the thumbtacks to mount the material on a rug frame, in a quilting hoop, or on artists' stretcher strips constructed so that they don't shift.

✷✷ KEEPING TRUE to the weave, cut the wool about 3/8" wide and 12" long and organize them in a basket according to color. Generally, the amount of wool needed to fill a blank space on the backing can be estimated to be strips cut from a piece of fabric that covers the space with four or five thicknesses.

✷✷ HOOKING IS A VERY SIMPLE technique that anyone can do with a little practice. Using a rug hook, which resembles a crochet hook with a wooden handle, you hold the strip of wool beneath the frame with your left hand and poke the hook from the top into the backing fabric with your right hand. Catch the strip onto the barb of the hook and draw it up through the fabric to create a 3/8"–high loop. Release and repeat this motion right beside the first loop. Continue until you have a "caterpillar" of loops in a row and reach the end of the strip or the space you want to fill. You do not have to hook through every hole. In fact, you can't, or the work will be too crowded. Think of creating a rug pile that is uniform and yet flexible to the design. The beginning and ending tail ends of the strip must be kept on the top of the work to lock the strip in place. Clip the ends to match the height of the other loops. You can go in any direction, but do not cross over other strips or twist the wool strip as you work. When you look on the back of the work, it should be smooth; on top, the backing should not show through.

✷✷ WHEN YOU HAVE COMPLETED the design, finish with two even rows all around the outside. Remove the work from the frame. Build up the footstool top with a few layers of quilt batting or pillow stuffing so that it has a soft base. Then place the finished work over it, judging for fit once more. It is easier to add or subtract stuffing filler to make it fit than it is to adjust the hooking. Trim the burlap backing to one inch all around the finished edge, fold the extra under 1/2", and staple or tack the work to the stool top evenly all around. Glue the gimp fringe over the staples so that it hangs down over the side of the stool edges.

rags and rugs

People are often surprised to hear that I make my rugs from old clothing, but that is the way the craft originated two hundred years ago. To colonial women and their European ancestors, woven fabric was difficult to come by and treasured in any form. So much of a woman's life was devoted to maximizing her resources for the home that it is no surprise to find that a piece of fabric, perhaps the mere collar on a jacket, was held so dear.

MANY SCRAPS were pieced and quilted into patchwork quilts, but sturdier pieces of wool were better suited for rag rugs. The word *rugg* actually referred to a bed covering, and indeed, most rugs were originally made as bed coverings. Over time, however, the rug found its way to the floor as a decorative covering over cold, bare wood or even hard-packed earth.

Imported rugs were too costly for most households, and the thrift of reusing rag bits combined with the need for decoration and personal artistic expression. Using a charred stick, women drew designs on old burlap feedsacks and used homemade hooks from horseshoe nails to pull rag strips through the holes in the burlap to render their designs. Designs began to take on the flavor of a region, their patterns inspired by the countryside, seascape, barnyard, or home.

The simplicity of the craft made it accessible to all, and the making of a rug became a family activity. Often a rug frame would be set up in the center of the home for months at a time. Everyone was invited—and, indeed, expected—to help with the task. Children came in with friends after school to help cut up rags or work at the rug itself. Like a quilt frame, the rug frame became a place to congregate—sharing skills, labor, and news.

Even now that necessity has given way to hobby, the craft of rug making still lends itself to cooperative work. Mothers and daughters can work together at an easy pace, leaving the work for other pursuits as they must. Many mothers have discovered that their children's artwork can be transferred to burlap and hooked in colorful detail. The naive perspective of a child's drawing is especially charming and appropriate for a rug design when rendered this way. Whether your daughter designs the rug, cuts the rags into strips, or takes on the hooking, any contribution to the project is sure to add sentimental value for both of you.

easel clock

Papier-mâché doesn't always have to be decorated with brightly colored whimsy. It is suitable to a more sophisticated design approach as well, which is the look that twenty-one-year-old Erin prefers in her college apartment. ◈◈◈ This wall or desk clock is quite simple as far as technique and materials, but the finish work uses decoupage to create an elegant, old world feeling. The image at the center of the dial is a favorite china saucer placed onto a copy machine and copied onto ivory paper. ◈◈◈ You could use any dish you love—or perhaps an old engraving, valentine, or black-and-white photograph. Remember, though, that when the clock mechanism is installed, the center will be obscured. ◈◈◈ If you each have different favorites, make two clocks. Working together, you can compare notes and help each other with discoveries and decisions along the way.

THIS TIME, LIKE ALL TIMES, IS A VERY GOOD ONE,
IF WE BUT KNOW WHAT TO DO WITH IT.

— RALPH WALDO EMERSON —

aggie made her own version of this clock by decoupaging the whole surface with photos and magazine cutouts about her best friend. It made an exceptional birthday gift. Erin took hers to college, and I made another just for the fun of it. The ledge is perfect for notes, mail, or a few favorite antique postcards.

you will need

TO MAKE ONE EASEL CLOCK:
- A PIECE OF CORRUGATED CARDBOARD 16″ X 12″
- SCRAPS FOR THE EASEL STAND AND LEDGE
- NEWSPAPER STRIPS
- FLOUR PASTE (SEE PAGE 84)
- WHITE PAINT
- GOLD TISSUE PAPER
- COPY OF AN OLD DOCUMENT
- COPY OF A FAVORITE 5″ SAUCER OR OTHER IMAGE
- 12 BUTTONS, PEBBLES, OR BEADS
- CLOCK MECHANISM WITH 2″ HANDS (CRAFT STORE) AND A BATTERY
- A SHORT (5″) LENGTH OF RIBBON
TOOLS:
- CUTTING MAT AND BOX CUTTER OR CRAFT KNIFE, DECOUPAGE MEDIUM, WHITE GLUE

◆ ENLARGE AND TRANSFER the clock base pattern from page 160 to the cardboard and place your selected image onto the clock base where shown on the pattern to see how it fits. Adjust either the clock base itself or the central image to form a pleasing combination. You might have to enlarge or reduce the dish copy to get a balanced look. Mark the clock center on all pieces. Cut the clock base out of the cardboard piece and the ledge shape as well. Cut a 5″ × 7″ rectangle for the easel stand. Cut a small X at the clock center. Use a pencil to create a hole that fits your clock mechanism comfortably. Tape the ledge onto the base where the base pattern indicates.

◆ PAPIER-MÂCHÉ ALL SIDES and allow to dry overnight or in a warm oven for about two hours. Repeat for a second layer. Stay mindful of

the thickness that your clock mechanism is restricted to: mine was designed for a 1/4" thickness. Take care to leave the center hole clean and free of papier-mâché. When dry, temporarily insert the clock mechanism into the hole and then tape the easel stand to the back of the clock just below the mechanism. Remove the mechanism and papier-mâché the stand to the back along the top edge only.

◆ **TWIST A LENGTH** of tissue and glue it to the top edge of the clock to form the scroll work. Paint all surfaces white. When dry (about thirty minutes), use decoupage medium to cover the clock with torn strips of gold tissue. Use your finger to burnish the strips and don't worry about overlapping, tearing, crinkling, or occasional gaps. This creates the faux finish of gold leaf and plaster.

◆ **WHEN DRY** (about ten minutes), trim your backing paper (a copy of an old document, letter, or whatever you prefer) to fit the interior pattern from page 160. Apply with decoupage medium. Allow to dry (another five minutes or so), then apply the central face image, making sure that the hole for the mechanism is correctly lined up. (When we applied our face, the copier ink broke down and smeared a bit onto the document backing. To disguise this obvious smudge, I took a pencil lead and smudged the document in other places to match—so it looked even older and better.)

◆ **WHEN EVERYTHING DRIES** (five to ten minutes), place the clock flat on the table and glue the buttons in place to indicate numerals. Allow to dry several hours, then install the mechanism and battery according to the manufacturer's instructions. Glue the ribbon to the easel back to keep it from slipping. If you choose to hang the clock on the wall instead, use the built-in hanger in the clock mechanism.

Collect buttons indiscriminately; hoard them. You never know when you will need them.

Send snapshots or clips to a daughter who lives away from home. Make the same project while apart and compare the results when you get together again.

- - - - - -

RECIPE SCRAPBOOK

HOOKED RUG

DECOUPAGED CHEST

as long as it takes

This chapter is about making things together that take a considerable amount of time. The projects that follow are designed to cover all sorts of skills, uses, and styles, but they do not have to be made start to finish in a single sitting—not even in several. Rather, they invite you to linger over the pleasure of the craft.

HAVE CONFIDENCE THAT IF YOU HAVE DONE A LITTLE THING WELL,
YOU CAN DO A BIGGER THING WELL, TOO.

— ANONYMOUS —

PATCHWORK QUILT

PAGE

140

PAPIER-MÂCHÉ DOLLHOUSE

PAGE

146

PAPIER-MÂCHÉ DOG HOUSE

PAGE

151

RECIPE SCRAPBOOK

INTERIOR

Contemplate the delightful treasure beneath your brush or needle—and the time you have set aside to share with your mother or daughter.

This is the chance to use all the things you have stashed away and wanted to find a good use for someday. Maybe you have a garage full of flea market finds, a drawer full of family recipes, a trunk stuffed with old wool clothes to cut up. Perhaps you have actually saved all those dearly sentimental baby dresses for this chance to piece them into a quilted scrapbook of your home life. But if all you have to work with are a few squares of felt from the dime store, it will still be an heirloom. When you make it together, mother and daughter, the heart and soul of the project shine through with an enormous brilliance only increased by time.

Remember that a large part of the charm of these projects lies in the imperfections and mistakes. They are the real-life legends of each heirloom. Just picture your little girl telling her own daughter someday, "I made this with my mother when I was seven. This is where I sewed the first patch on upside down. So we put away the pattern and just decided to make our own design. Weren't we clever?"

recipe scrapbook

Looking through your recipe box or file you will surely see recipes that are like snapshots of your life at home. The handwritten cards are especially precious for all the memories the writing itself evokes. We have several that reflect the food favorites at our house—the year of the cherry tart, the butter ball cookies the girls make for my birthday, and "Pancakes Our Way." ◆◆◆ The cards are well worn, but seem like little voices from the past, and I treasure every smudgey stain and imperfect letter. When we collected them in this scrapbook, we looked for school pictures and other clippings to include. Maury thought her Smoothie recipe looked so wonderful on the page that she was inspired to continue the scrapbook pages with new recipes and decorations. ◆◆◆ Even as a blank book with a handmade decorated cover, this would make a wonderful gift for a bride, new mother, or grandmother who will love to fill the pages with her vision of family.

MEMORY IS TO LOVE WHAT THE SAUCER IS TO THE CUP.

— ELIZABETH BOWEN —

FOR THE COVER, cut a panel of a decorative gift wrap paper to size plus an inch on the top, bottom, and right side. Apply the cut paper to the front with the adhesive and, after clipping excess corner paper, wrap the edges to the inside of the cover. Add a decorative label to the center. You could hand-letter the label or use the computer to print one with a photocopied letter for background. A bold typeface will stand out nicely against the pattern. Add any cutouts or accent trims you have selected for the cover. Use the decoupage medium to paint the cover (this adds a protective covering to the collage). A length of ribbon can be applied over the left edge of the paper cover.

ON THE INSIDE of the cover, apply a paper panel large enough to conceal the wrapped edges of the front cover. Cut this slightly smaller than the cover so that it doesn't show when the book is closed.

THE INTERIOR PAGES can be decorated in any way that you like. We used a plastic photo sleeve for a recipe card that was printed on both sides. That way it could be removed but kept safely inside the album. A homemade recipe card once sent as a Christmas card from our family fills the page on the left and is a good fit with a little bit of vintage shelf trim saved from our old house. Snapshots of children, dishes, and family celebrations can be photocopied and pasted inside for decoration with ribbon trims, cutouts, and stickers. Colored papers scalloped at the edges and dotted with a hole punch make quick border decorations. Encourage your daughter to write down her impressions of foods and recipes. Everyone will enjoy reviewing these entries through the years to come as the scrapbook fills with special favorites.

you will need

TO MAKE ONE SCRAPBOOK:
- A BLANK ARCHIVAL (ACID-FREE PAPER) SCRAPBOOK IN A SIZE THAT WORKS FOR YOUR NEEDS
- DECORATIVE PAPERS, RIBBONS, TRIMS, STICKERS, CUTOUTS
- ARCHIVAL PLASTIC SLEEVES FOR RECIPE CARDS PRINTED ON BOTH SIDES

TOOLS:
- ACID-FREE ADHESIVE TAPE, GLUE OR GLUE STICK, DECOUPAGE MEDIUM, SCISSORS, AND HOLE PUNCH

toni, kate, and mary

Toni is a food writer, cookbook author, and cooking teacher with two teenaged daughters, Kate and Mary. Both girls have applied their own talents to food in ways that have made their mother take note. Toni is sure that their success in the kitchen comes partly from her willingness to let their personalities take the lead. "Mary has always been a 'Me do it' type. She doesn't ask for help and wants to figure out everything for herself, even if it means doing it the hard way the first time.

COOKING MAY BE AS MUCH A MEANS OF SELF-EXPRESSION AS ANY OF THE ARTS.

FANNIE FARMER

WHEN SHE BAKED bread as a ten-year-old, it was Parker House rolls—lots of steps, but eventually, she got it right. My general feeling about cooking with kids is that ten minutes in the kitchen where the child is really engaged and doing something interesting is better than two hours where the mom is doing most of the work. Let your five-year-old cut shapes from the pastry dough—she can learn to make and roll it in a few years, when she will be more successful at that. Try not to hover or be too proprietary about the space. I've found it's better to let them make the big mess or try something different. That's where the creativity comes in and then the mastery follows. Trial and error help develop the skills that most of us take for granted."

All this experimenting has brought each of Toni's daughters to a point where she has family specialties of her own. "You can encourage your children to develop their own recipes. Teach them to make scrambled eggs, praise the results lavishly, and with practice they're likely to get pretty good at it." Kate makes a guacamole that she has adapted from her mother's original recipe, adding her own ingredients and techniques. "It's really very good and I don't even know what she puts in it now."

She realized when the girls returned from camp one summer that food is a powerful way of connecting a family. When Kate and Mary started requesting specific food favorites throughout the car ride home, Toni could see how important simple recipes become. She suggests writing them all down in a scrapbook for each, complete with children's sketches of favorite dishes or snapshots of fun in the kitchen and celebrations at the table. No doubt they will have lots to add on their own, but even now, so many years later, when Toni looks at her grandmother's handwritten recipe for cinnamon rolls, the memories are vividly summoned. Toni recalls with a smile that her grandmother "baked bread every day and made cinnamon rolls with part of the dough. I loved to watch her and to help. It doesn't even matter that she totally forgot to write down the cinnamon on the card." Toni knows exactly how to make them—it's pretty much all by heart.

hooked rug

My father-in-law once stood on this rug and asked where he might find the wool pants he had left in the guest room closet many years earlier, before he moved to the South Pacific. "They are right under your left shoe," I confessed. ◉◉◉ Bewildered, he looked down at the rug, slowly recognizing shapes of the same color and fabric he once wore as trousers. That yellow-brown flannel was delightful to hook into the rug and I wish I had more, but I would have to find a new source. Everyone knows better by now than to leave wool clothes unattended at my house for long. ◉◉◉ But the girls happily adopted the tale and still frequently ask when they look at the rug, "Where are Grampa's pants?" Which part did I do? is the next question, and so on until we have picked apart all the legends of the rug.

ANY ROAD IS BOUND TO ARRIVE SOMEWHERE IF YOU FOLLOW IT FAR ENOUGH.

— PATRICIA WENTWORTH —

A rug that is divided into blocks like this one gives everyone a chance to design or work on part of the project. The small areas allow for color changes or design adaptations that suit the designer whether she is four or forty. Most important, like the little footstool top described earlier, the blocks are completed simply and quickly so that everyone has the feeling of great accomplishment without investing too much time.

⊙⊙ **BEGIN BY WASHING** and drying the wool fabrics in small, like-color batches on the highest water level. Sort and cut some strips to have handy for starting. Transfer the rug pattern from page 159 to the rug backing fabric of your choice, using a marker and staying straight to the weave. Machine stitch around raw edges of fabric with two rows and cover the edge with masking tape to protect it from unraveling.

⊙⊙ **PLACE BACKING** in the rug frame with thumbtacks or in a quilting hoop with the center of the design to be worked first. Refer to the photograph for color decisions or adapt the colors you have to the design, especially when adding scraps that will bring a richness of tone to otherwise solid shapes. Alternating dark and light backgrounds in the squares is more important than matching shades exactly.

⊙⊙ **OCCASIONALLY STAND BACK** and look at the work to judge color values from a distance. Remove strips as needed and adjust to achieve the right effect. Choose a place (such as the basket front) to add your initials and the date. Some rug makers add a label to the back rather than hooking the information into the design.

⊙⊙ **AFTER THE DESIGN** is done, continue using the purple to make a single-line border, then two lines of green, and finish with another single line of purple. Trim the backing to 1″ all around, clipping corners diagonally. In the middle of one side edge, begin to hand-sew the rug tape to the backing right up against the finished edge of the rug, butting the two ends of the tape and sewing securely at the joint where they meet on the return. Fold the tape over and sew the remaining tape edge to the backing with a hemstitch so that it neatly covers the raw edge of the backing. Place the rug facedown on a towel and use a barely dampened press cloth and iron on a low setting to block the rug with a soft stamping motion.

◉◉ **NEVER WASH A RUG.** Vacuum lightly, spot clean with a damp rag, and refresh by turning it over on a snowy lawn, if possible. Wool is very durable and will take a good bit of foot traffic. Over time the pile will crush and the colors will fade somewhat. As part of the family life, it ages with us.

- - - - - -

Create a tool basket that is especially for your daughter so she has access to brushes, sewing supplies, scissors, and glue when she wants to work without you.

Plan a menu that gives you time to work. If you will be home all day, what could you make that fits your style? Soups, stews, and breads are good for home days.

- - - - - -

you will need

TO MAKE A HOOKED RUG MEASURING 28″ x 37″:
- RUG BURLAP OR MONK'S CLOTH BACKING FABRIC MEASURING 34″ x 43″
- 4 YARDS OF COTTON TWILL RUG TAPE 1 1/4″ TO 1 1/2″ WIDE
- MASKING TAPE

- PREWASHED WOOL FABRIC IN THESE APPROXIMATE AMOUNTS AND COLORS (BASED ON 60″ YARD GOODS):
  1/2 YARD DARK GREEN
  1/2 YARD TRUE RED
  1/8 YARD EACH OF PINK-BROWN TWEED, DUSTY ROSE, LIGHT GRAY, SKY-BLUE TWEED, BLUE-AND-WHITE PLAID, PINK-AND-WHITE PLAID, GRAY-GREEN PLAID, BLUE-GRAY PLAID, MUSTARDY YELLOW, MAUVE-PINK
  1/3 YARD PURPLE
  1/2 YARD LEAF GREEN
- SCRAPS IN RUST BROWN, DARK BROWN, DARK AND LIGHT GREENS, WHITE, PINKS, AND REDS
TOOLS:
- A RUG FRAME OR QUILT HOOP, THUMBTACKS, MARKER, RUG HOOK, SCISSORS, NEEDLE, AND STRONG THREAD

decoupaged chest

For a ragtag piece of furniture, this odd chest of drawers has led a full life. I thought a few dollars was a lot to pay for it at a garage sale, but it had flat surfaces that would be perfect for an experimental makeover. 🌷🌷🌷 We started out by repainting it, then we decorated it with colorful scenes using each drawer front as a separate canvas. That was fun, but a few years later, we gave it another look and decided to renovate again. This time, the easiest thing to do was to paper it with newsprint and decoupage it with copies of family photos and clip art I'd been collecting. 🌷🌷🌷 It has turned out to be such a favorite that I wish I had chosen a better-quality paper. The newsprint has yellowed a bit, but that cupboard has an amazing ability to steal the show time after time.

THERE'S ALWAYS ROOM FOR IMPROVEMENT—
IT'S THE BIGGEST ROOM IN THE HOUSE.

— LOUISE HEATH LEBER —

you will need

TO DECORATE A CUPBOARD OR
DRESSER:

- A CLEAN PIECE OF FURNITURE THAT
  HAS A FEW FLAT SURFACES
- NEWSPRINT LIKE THE FINANCIAL
  PAGES OR CLASSIFIEDS WITH
  SMALLISH, EVEN PRINT
- AN ASSORTMENT OF IMAGES TO
  COPY IN BLACK AND WHITE USING
  IVORY COPY PAPER
- GOLD TISSUE PAPER AND GOLD
  ACRYLIC PAINT

TOOLS:

- DECOUPAGE MEDIUM, BRUSHES,
  SCISSORS, ACRYLIC SEALER

ONCE THE PIECE is cleaned up, cut pieces of newsprint to fit the panels in a patchwork or consider copying a few of these onto ivory copy paper for a longer lasting quality. Apply decoupage medium to the backs of the newsprint pieces and apply them to the piece. Carefully smooth out air bubbles and pieces that overlap each other. Be sure to wrap the paper neatly inside the drawer edges. Allow to dry (thirty minutes to an hour).

BEGIN TO COPY, clip, and paste on family photographs, artwork from old books, favorite quotes, and clips from magazines. Apply in a random fashion. Everyone in the family can have a turn. There always seems to be room for more additions, and we have treated this project as an ongoing scrapbook. Just put glue on the back of a cutout and stick it on. As long as they are all black-and-white copies on the same ivory-colored paper, they will go together quite well. We used gold paint to cover the mismatched drawer pulls and gold tissue to add a border at the bottom and along a drawer edge. When you have finished, protect the work with a coat of sealer, but we have had good luck adding images even after this final step and spot coating with the sealer there again.

- - - - - -

Keep an accordion file nearby for magazine clips,
greeting cards, wraps, and images
to store for collages and decoupage later.

Go to a museum, a house tour, or an artist's studio
for inspiration. Share your notes and recollections
over lunch. Ask yourselves, "What could we do
that would be like that?"

- - - - - -

kathy and hayley

It isn't an accident that ten-year-old Hayley likes to make quilts with her mother. "I kept my quilt frame set up in the living room with an old quilt in it and encouraged each of my children to play around it, hide and seek, a playhouse for trucks and dolls, whatever they wanted to do there. From the very beginning, I wanted to create a strong memory and fondness for quilting.

I LOVE QUILTING and spend a great deal of my time designing and constructing quilts. Naturally, I have always looked for ways to grow that enthusiasm in my sons and daughter, too," explains Kathy, an award-winning quilt designer

Following the tradition established by her big brothers, Travis and Jordan, Hayley designed and directed the construction of her first quilt when she was three. Even then Hayley had a distinctive style and color sense of her own that tested Kathy's own instincts. "She wanted to use a shade of green that I never would have chosen. But I bit my tongue and held back my disapproval. I kept reminding myself that it was her quilt, her decision, and I knew it was more important to let her do it her way. The finished quilt was so alive and full of energy— all from that unusual color. It was such an inspiration to me that in every quilt I have made since, I use a little bit of that color. From then on, I trusted her judgment."

Many quilts later, Kathy and Hayley have created an occasional evening tradition referred to as "We Girls Together." Given the opportunity to be just girls, they will head for Kathy's studio at home and get right to work on the project of the moment. Here, Hayley has her own ready-to-go basket of supplies and inspiration aplenty to strike a creative spark. Although she would never try to change Hayley's mind, Kathy finds that it's a good idea to put out a few suggestions and then narrow the field of possibilities to get the project off the ground. Inspired by a new teddy bear in need of a special quilt or perhaps just a handful of beautiful fabrics, a miniature flower quilt for a vintage bear takes hold in Hayley's imagination. As they work to execute her design, Hayley will ask her mother for stories of her childhood or dreams of other things they might do together as she grows up. "It's a fantasy come true," confesses Kathy. "This is what I hoped we would do together. At first I just wanted her to understand and value what I do, but it turns out that she loves to make quilts, too—and she wants to make them with me."

WHAT AN ENORMOUS MAGNIFIER IS TRADITION! HOW A THING GROWS IN THE HUMAN MEMORY AND IN THE HUMAN IMAGINATION, WHEN LOVE, WORSHIP, AND ALL THAT LIES IN THE HUMAN HEART, IS THERE TO ENCOURAGE IT.

———

THOMAS CARLYLE

patchwork quilt

I am not much of a quilter. My pieces don't always match up precisely, and my quilting stitches look awfully big compared to some. ✕✕✕ I do, however, have a good sense of color and pattern, and that is what I try to share with my daughters when we work together. Add in the communal creativity that occurs when a project like this one fills the house (I use the dining room table as a work space) and it becomes a wonderful activity to share. No matter how it turns out in the end, a quilt is always treasured, even if it winds up bunched around the Christmas tree stand once a year. ✕✕✕ I have made quilts by myself, but those made with my daughters have been far more interesting and successful. To have another eye, opinion, and pair of hands at work on the construction of a quilt has obvious merit.

MAKE THE MOST OF YOURSELF, FOR THAT IS ALL THERE IS OF YOU.

— RALPH WALDO EMERSON —

A contribution as small as the selection of fabrics becomes larger in meaning as the patch-work comes together and the colors begin to create a kaleidoscope of pattern. In the case of this very simple patch quilt, we decided to eliminate a color after the pieces were cut. Those orphaned squares found their way into a little doll's quilt built while we took breaks from the larger project.

Cutting, sewing, and quilting go so much faster when there are helpers. There is something for everyone to contribute here. Just be sure to maintain the momentum that you establish in the beginning—which doesn't mean to suggest that the project should take a crazed precedence over all else. If you find that you need the dining table for a sit-down dinner, by all means, set the quilt aside. But don't bury it in a box under the

bed. In view nestled in a lovely basket, it has a better chance of being revived and completed. Your daughter might even be the one to insist.

✖ ✖ BEGIN BY WASHING and drying the fabrics. Press the wrinkles out before cutting. Make a template of cardboard measuring 5¹/4″ by 5¹/4″. Fold each length of cotton in thirds lengthwise, selvage to selvage, and place on the cutting mat. Place the template at one end with room on all sides. Cut away the selvage. Use the rotary cutter and steel ruler to cut through all three thicknesses, but be careful not to trim cardboard off the template as well. Cut squares exactly the size of the template You will be cutting 306 squares—17 each of 18 fabrics. Stack these and set aside.

you will need

FOR A FULL-SIZE BED QUILT
MEASURING 86" x 78":

- 1/2 YARD EACH OF EIGHTEEN TO
  TWENTY DIFFERENT COTTON
  FABRICS
- CARDBOARD FOR A TEMPLATE
- 90" x 108" BATTING
- 6 YARDS BACKING FABRIC

TOOLS:

- SEWING MACHINE, THREAD, PINS,
  SCISSORS, QUILT HOOP, QUILTING
  THREAD, QUILTING NEEDLE
  ("BETWEENS"), IRON AND IRONING
  BOARD, ROTARY FABRIC CUTTER,
  STEEL RULER, CUTTING MAT

✖ ✖ ON A TABLE, lay the squares edge to edge, alternating lights and darks, to achieve the width of the quilt. At the sewing machine, with the edges of two pieces matched perfectly and pinned together, sew a straight seam of 3/8". If your machine does not have a marker to indicate that measurement, place a piece of tape there. Maury, my eleven-year-old, did most of the seaming once she realized that all she had to watch for was the fabric edge against the marker. They all turned out perfectly. Instead of clipping threads at the ending of each seam, keep running pairs of patches through the machine in the order of your earlier layout. They end up like flags on a line, and it is easier to clip all threads at the end of the entire set of patches. Then sew the right edge of each pair of patches to the left edge of the next pair until you have one continuous strip of patches the full width of the quilt. If the strip appears to be crooked in any place, undo the seam with a seam ripper and resew for accuracy. Trim seam allowances to 1/8" and press all seam allowances to one side.

Lay the strip on the table and place another row of patches beside the strip you have completed. Consider the fabrics as they look beside each other, lights and darks balanced with patterns. Sew this strip together as you did the last. Trim, press, and correct if needed. Place this strip right side against

- - - - - -

An old quilt can inspire colors and patterns
to mix together. Perhaps you have old baby
dresses or scraps from early sewing
projects that you can use for this. Your daughter
or mother will enjoy selecting the fabrics
and planning the design with you.

- - - - - -

the first and pin at every seam, being sure that the seams meet exactly. Sew the two strips together. Trim and press the seam allowance to one side.

Continue in this way until you have a quilt top that measures eighteen squares by seventeen squares, or whatever dimension you prefer.

✱✱ **WASH AND PRESS** the backing fabric. Cut into two lengths and divide the second length down the center into two pieces. Sew each halved piece to one side of the first full length. This method avoids having a seam straight down the middle of the backing fabric. A seam at each edge of a central panel (close to the edge of the mattress) is preferable. Press. Place the backing fabric wrong side up on a large flat surface like the dining room table. Open the batting and place on top. Place

the quilt top on top of all this, right side up. Center the top so that it sits squarely on the batting and backing, which should be at least 4½″ larger all around than the pieced top. Be sure that the excess backing fabric is evenly distributed around the edges and that the seams on the backing fabric run parallel to the quilt top. Use large safety pins to secure the three layers all around the edges and in the center of the quilt at regular intervals 12″ apart. Roll the backing up over the exposed batting to neaten it and pin it closed.

✱✱ **PLACE THE QUILT** inside a hoop and begin at the center to quilt the layers together. We quilted diagonally through each square, but you could choose any quilt pattern you like. Move the hoop as you need to until you have quilted all the squares according to your pattern. Keep knots inside seams and backstitch to finish rather than knot. When finished quilting, trim the batting 2″ larger than the quilt top and the backing to an even 4½″ width all around and fold the raw edge of the backing in ½″. Press and then fold the backing over to the front of the quilt. Pin in place for a 2″ border and binding. Hemstitch securely, mitering the corners neatly.

\- - - - - -

Keep a journal of wishes, dreams, and possibilities. Sharing these while you work will intensify the memory.

Rent an old movie that you think your daughter might not choose on her own. Watch it while you work or afterward.

Set up a specific time and place for the next session. Put it on the calendar. Plan for the day with cookies, tea, and materials.

\- - - - - -

quilting

Patchwork quilting is perhaps the best known traditional mother-daughter craft. In America, colonial women had a limited supply of fabric that was either imported at great expense or woven at home with great effort. When a worn spot appeared in a blanket or bed covering, a careful patch was applied. Over time, the original blanket became a foundation for an entire joined patchwork of artistic patches and stitches.

MANY WOMEN used this early "crazy quilt" as a schoolroom for a daughter's sewing instruction. Sewing was an important skill and was taken very seriously by both mother and daughter. Under a mother's watchful eye, stitches were practiced daily. Although their task was to maintain the comfort of the household, examples of personal artistry and tradition found their way through the needle as well. Through the years, uniquely intricate patterns built from pieces of fabric salvaged from worn clothing created a kind of family history embellished with beautiful embroidery and ultimately cherished as an irreplaceable heirloom.

In later periods of history, patchwork developed into piecework. This still emphasized economy with its small scraps of material, but now the pieces were collected, designed, cut into uniform shapes, and pieced together to create a pattern. This piecework pattern or quilt top became the top layer of a quilted "sandwich" with cotton batting in the middle and a length of woven fabric as backing. The three layers were then stretched onto a large frame and sewn together in patterned stitches through all layers to make a finished quilt—thick, warm, and pleasing to the eye. Young children often played on the floor under the broad canopy of the quilt frame. Women and older daughters who worked at the edges would ask the little ones to pass up a lost needle or tell of sloppy work seen beneath.

Women often made quilts to celebrate important family events. The birth of a baby, a wedding, a son's coming of age—each was an occasion to create a beautiful quilt. It was common for a daughter to piece a number of quilt tops in her years of sewing at home, each a bit more complicated than the last. The last top was expected to be her best work, the wedding quilt for her marriage bed. Before her wedding, all the community women would gather together and quilt her collection of tops into finished quilts for her hope chest, creating comfort for a new life away from home. Once there, the bride would set up her quilting frame and continue the tradition.

papier-mâché dollhouse

There is something about a dollhouse that makes just about any girl of any age fall into starry daydreams of tinkering and fussing over very small things in very small rooms. This project took much longer than it needed to, mostly because there was a great deal of imagining along the way. Indeed, that was perhaps the best part, and there was no need to rush those sweet moments when all things seemed possible. ❧ ❧ ❧ Maury and I sketched out a number of simple cottages, but in the end we created a palace of sorts. Our family house of houses was the pink Victorian that all three girls grew up in, and I'm afraid that for years to come all our fantasy houses will have to be pink—very pink. This one, then, is predictably so, but the color is well chosen for this yummy creation.

JOY IS THE VERY DISTILLED ELIXIR OF ENERGY AND INSPIRATION.

— LILIAN WHITING —

P ainting it and dressing it up felt like decorating a birthday cake, a finger-licking froth of raspberry, peppermint, and buttercream frosting. No matter that it was paint and paper, it was still delicious.

Note — The paint box will be the main structure for the house.

☼ CUT THE TOP OFF the box and save this piece. Cut away the inner box flaps and reseal any openings at the sides. Reinforce well with tape. Stand the box on one side.

☼ CUT THE RESERVED cardboard to fit into the box for a second floor. Pencil mark spots on the back wall, upstairs and downstairs, for windows and a door. Remove the floor insert, set it aside, and then carefully cut out the windows and door. Save the door. Replace the floor, being careful to keep it level, and securely tape into place. Where necessary, use poster board or thin cardboard to

create an extra floor layer covering that will be smooth. (We did this at the top of the box, now the third floor, because the original box closure left a dent that would have made it hard to stand furniture on it. The bottom wasn't as bad and was stabilized by the base, but it might be needed there, too.)

☼ MAKE THE PASTE by mixing 1 cup warm water, 1/2 cup flour, and 1 tablespoon white glue. (You will have to remix batches of paste as you go along, but keep to these proportions. As you work, the paste accumulates burs of paper that roughen the finish. It's good to start fresh from time to time.) Mix with your fingers to the smooth consistency of heavy cream. Dip torn strips of newspaper into the paste, slide the strips between your fingers to remove excess paste, and apply to box walls and floors, wrapping at edges of windows or walls. Before you do this, choose a few books that fit the

opening between the floors (the height of the walls) and wrap them in plastic wrap. Stand them up inside the house while the first layer is drying to keep the second floor from sagging or warping.

✿ WHEN THIS STAGE IS DRY, cut a triangle (11″ x 11″ x 13 1/2″) for the third floor pitch. Bend it 3/4″ from the edge along the long side. Check it for fit and cut out the third-floor window. Tape onto the dry box top, which is the floor for the third floor. Cut out roof sides (two rectangles measuring 9″ x 14″) and tape these together along the pitch. Then tape the roof to the triangle, careful to keep edges in line, but allow for a 3/4″ overhang on the front of the house. Use straight pins to keep the roof pieces in place at the open side of the house or they will droop. Tape securely wherever possible. Papier-mâché this section now and let dry. Then papier-mâché all surfaces again. Allow to dry and repeat with another layer. Papier-mâché dries very hard, and the number of layers you add is discretionary. We thought three layers was sufficient for strength and appearance, but you could certainly add more. That depends upon the patience you

you will need

TO MAKE ONE DOLLHOUSE:
- A PAINT BOX CARTON THAT HELD 4 GALLONS OF PAINT, ABOUT 13″ x 13″ x 8″
- EXTRA CORRUGATED BOXES TO CUT UP FOR BASE, ROOF, AND DETAILS
- SHIRT OR POSTER BOARD FOR DETAILS
- PASTE MADE FROM FLOUR, WATER, AND WHITE GLUE
- NEWSPAPER STRIPS
- PAPIER-MÂCHÉ PULP
- POTATOES
- DOILIES, SMALL FLOWERS AND LEAVES, CLAY POT, AND DOWEL

TOOLS:
- SANDPAPER, MASKING TAPE, BOX CUTTER, CRAFT KNIFE, CUTTING MAT, RULER, PINS, PAINTS, BRUSHES, SEALER

have for this process. (Each layer should dry overnight.)

✿ MAKE WINDOW BOXES according to the patterns and add them to the house with tape and strips to windows as desired. For shutters, cut rectangles out of cardboard with the corrugation running horizontally. Then use the knife to cut just through the top layer of paper 1/8″ from the edge to create an inset shutter area. Peel the paper away to reveal rippled corrugation beneath. Pick off any paper that doesn't come away easily, but the paint process will smooth the rough surface of the corrugation. Papier-mâché the flat edges at the sides

smooth seal. Place the house and base onto a magazine that is centered under the house. Then weight the base at all four corners so it dries flat. Move the weights to allow all areas to dry as needed.

✿ **MAKE THE FENCE** by using the pattern from page 160. Papier-mâché the fence on all sides for strength before attaching to the house and base. Attach it to the house with tape at the edges and at the feet of the long posts, which you have bent to rest on the base. (This should dry overnight, also.)

✿ **WHEN EVERYTHING** is totally dry, lightly sand the edges and surfaces for a smooth surface free of burs. Paint the shutters and the entire structure inside and out with white paint. If there are any areas that look weak, rough, or poorly papered, repaper them now and repaint when dry. Two coats of white paint will hide the newspaper print. I like it to show through a little so that the folksy handmade feeling stays.

- - - - - -

Fool around with the materials to experiment.
The first attempt doesn't have to be perfection.
It might take a few tries.

- - - - - -

and backs, but do not cover the interior, which is meant to resemble louvers. Take the reserved front door and trim its edges to be a bit smaller than the opening. Cut out a little window and papier-mâché all edges like the shutters.

✿ **CUT OUT** the 17″ × 17″ base and papier-mâché both sides. When dry, apply ample glue to the bottom of the house. Set it onto the base and weight the inside of the house with canned goods to keep it flat while drying. When dry, papier-mâché the sides of the base again and wrap the strips up the side of the house for a secure and

✿ **PAINT AND DECORATE** your house in the colors and patterns of your choice. You could wallpaper the walls with decorative paper and add curtains snipped from doilies as we did. Potato stamps created interesting floor, wall, and grass patterns. We also made topiary trees, shrubs, and pines out of papier-mâché pulp mixed with water and sculpted into these forms. And then there is furniture, also a great way to continue the project by making little tables, chairs, sofas, beds...whatever comes to mind. And, of course, people are needed for a dollhouse, too.

One day long after the dollhouse was complete, Maury and her friend Anne Marie stood admiring the beautiful little house. Maury told her all about the details of making it, the fun she had watching it come together. "I wish we could make it again," she said with a sigh. After a pause, she added with a sweet, wishful smile, "Can we?" I was tempted to say yes, thinking that I shouldn't miss an opportunity to encourage this kind of thing, but it was a big project.

a house for pugsly

A bit more than I thought we should take on in an afternoon. How could we modify it to be a smaller undertaking? A playhouse for the dollhouse? Another simpler design—shoe box size? A doghouse for stuffed animals? The doghouse was the winning idea, and, indeed, it was perfect. In half an hour, I helped them construct two simple sheds, each with just one cutout opening for a door. Then they spent a few hours layering papier-mâché strips, letting their excitement and paint design plans race ahead while they waited for the

drying. In the same afternoon they were able to paint and decorate and even play with the twin houses.

And I just watched. Maury knew enough by now to guide the project step by step. Suddenly a boring "home day" was full of energy and fun. The little houses turned out so well; they were adorable, and the girls were quite proud of them. I saw that all this "crafting" at home had another payoff. Maury could do this *without* me, too. Someday she will teach her children to look for fun in an old cardboard box and a stack of newspaper. I wonder what they will make.

sources

rug hooking

Harry M. Fraser Co.
P.O. Box 939
Stoneville, NC 27048
336-573-9830
FraserRugs@aol.com

supplies, patterns, strip cutters, catalog for mail order

Forestheart Studio
200 South Main Street
Woodsboro, MD 21798
301-845-4447
foresthrt@aol.com

supplies, books, kits, videos, beads, ribbons, fiber arts, catalog for mail order

Holly Berry Hill
480 Abbie Street
Pleasonton, CA 94566
877-424-4455
hollybhill@aol.com

mail order catalog for supplies, patterns, doll making kits

The Robin's Nest
2359 Highway 58
Buffalo Junction, VA 24529
804-374-HOOK
robinsnest@kerrlake.com

complete line of rug hooking supplies including the Hasty Lap and floor frames

The Wool Barn
P.O. Box 249
Dayton, TX 77535
409-257-9338
palders@lcc.net

supplies, patterns, catalog for mail order ($5)

doll making

Magic Cabin Dolls
1950 Waldorf, NW
Grand Rapids, MI 49550
888-623-6557

felt, doll kits, patterns, tools, yarn, dollhouse accessories

A Child's Dream
P.O. Box 1499
Boulder, CO 80306-1499
800-359-2906

doll making supplies, wool felt, tools, fabrics

Creative Hands
P.O. Box 2217
Eugene, OR 97402
541-343-1562

wool felt, dolls, kits, materials

general crafts

Note: Most materials are available through a local craft, art, or hardware store.

Walnut Hollow
1409 State Road 23
Dodgeville, WI
53533-2122
800-950-5101

wood products and accessories, clock movements and accessories

Creative Beginnings
P.O. Box 1330
Morro Bay, CA 93442
800-367-1739
www.creative-beginnings.com

jewelry findings, charms, beads, catalog for mail order ($5)

Dover Publications, Inc.
31 East Second Street
Mineola, NY 11501

clip art collections

Plaid Enterprises, Inc.
800-392-8673
(or 800-842-4197 for technical support)

acrylic craft paints, Mod Podge, decoupage medium, and accessories

Offray Ribbons
800-344-5533

JoAnn Fabrics and Crafts
888-739-4120

Binney and Smith
110 Church Street
Easton, PA 18044

Liquitex brand acrylic paints and sealers

Kate's Paperie
561 Broadway
New York, NY 10012
800-809-9880

paper products and scrapbook materials

Exposures
P.O. Box 3615
Oshkosh, WI 54903
800-572-5750

photo frames and albums

s t i t c h   g u i d e

blanket stitch

cross stitch

french knot

running stitch

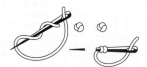

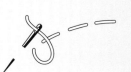

glossary

Acetate Plastic sheets sold in tablets available at the art or office supply store.

Acrylic paints and sealer Water-based paints that are widely available, easy to use, and inexpensive.

Batting The lofted, puffy filling inside a quilt. Available at all fabric stores in a variety of dimensions.

Blanket stitch A decorative edge stitch created by inserting the needle 1/4" from the fabric edge, bringing it beneath the fabric to catch the thread before repeating the stitch 1/4" to the right. (See diagram.)

Craft knife A sharp, pointed knife blade embedded in a handle for intricate cutting.

Cross-stitch A decorative sewing stitch made by combining two diagonal stitches to form an X. The first stitch is made going lower right to top left and completed by laying over a stitch from bottom left to top right.

Cutting mat A self-healing, synthetic cutting mat designed specifically to receive sharp cuts from a rotary or craft knife.

Craft burlap Inexpensive burlap fabric with a rough, irregular weave.

Decoupage medium Adhesive formulated for paper decoupage. Alternatives include white glue, Mod Podge, artist's gesso, gel medium, or wallpaper paste.

Drying time Varies according to amount of moisture in the product, the air, and the application.

Embroidery floss Most common embroidery thread available. Generally made from six strands, it can be separated for a variety of thicknesses.

Felting A process that binds wool fibers together after exposure to heat, agitation, and moisture. Achieved by placing wool fabric or knitted material in a washing machine full of hot water and running through a wash cycle. Further felting occurs in the dryer, if desired.

French knot A sewing stitch whereby the needle is held close to the fabric at the point where it was brought up through the fabric. Wrap the thread around the needle two or three times. Reinsert the needle beside the exit point so that a heavy knot is formed when the thread wraps slip off the needle and are anchored by the stitch.

Iron-on bonding product Also called fusible webbing. Follow manufacturer's instructions to bond to fabric using heat from an iron.

Pearl cotton A twisted, corded floss in a variety of gauges numbered 3, 5, 8, and 12.

Quilting stitch A running stitch used to bind the layers of a quilt together. (See also Running stitch.)

Right sides together Top side of fabric design placed facing each other so that after seaming, seam will be hidden on the back when opened flat.

Rotary fabric cutter A wheel-shaped knife with a handle that allows smooth, straight cutting on a protective mat.

Rug burlap and monk's cloth Foundation material for hooked rug making. Available through catalogs and rug supply shops. Differs from craft burlap in fiber strength and regular weave.

Rug hook A hook that resembles a crochet hook set into a wooden handle. Used to hook wool strips through a foundation material.

Running stitch A small sewing stitch through all layers of fabric. Several stitches may be taken on the needle before pulling it through.

Seam allowance Additional fabric needed when sewing two pieces together. 3/8" is the general width assumed to allow.

Selvage Factory woven edge on sides of fabric lengthwise.

Transfer pen Used to transfer a design from paper to fabric, following manufacturer's instructions. Ink disappears over a short time.

Wool yarn Also called crewel wool or Persian yarn, it comes in small bundles for needlepoint and embroidery work.

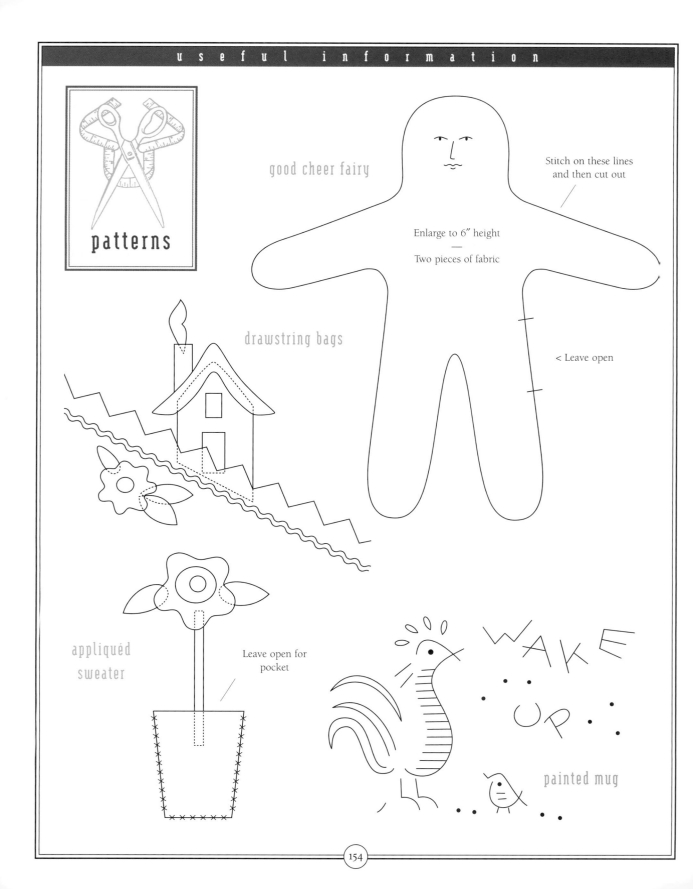

patterns

good cheer fairy

Stitch on these lines
and then cut out

Enlarge to 6″ height
—
Two pieces of fabric

< Leave open

drawstring bags

appliquéd
sweater

Leave open for
pocket

painted mug

paper lace

Transfer design to
folded paper

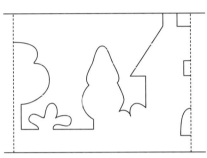

< Dotted lines indicate folds

painted mug

painted mug

painted mug

tea cozy

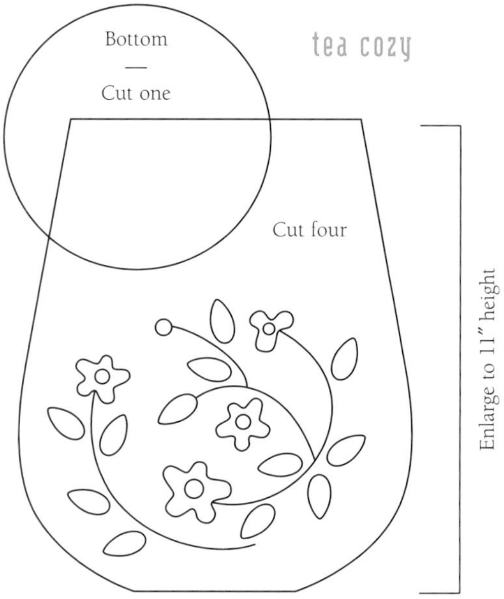

Bottom
—
Cut one

Cut four

Enlarge to 11" height

cookie candle box

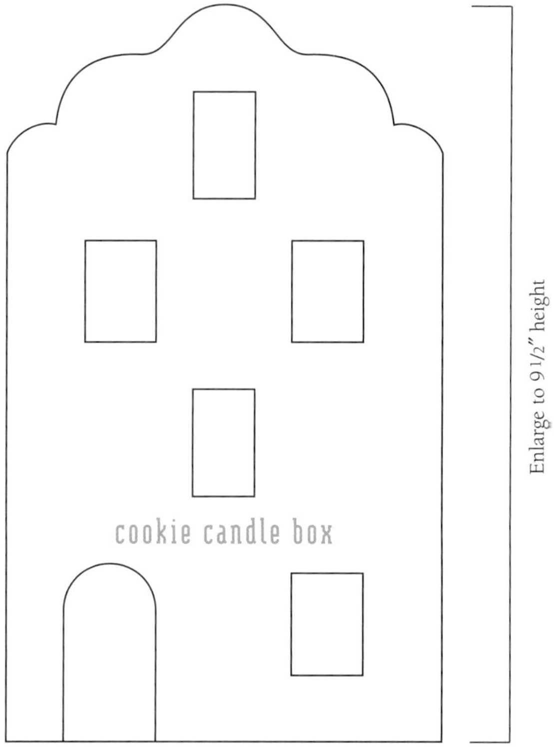

Enlarge to 9 1/2" height

A   Attach ear

Head side
—
Cut two

teddy bear

Body
—
Cut two

Enlarge to 9" height

Head back
—
Cut one

Ear
—
Cut two

Pleat

< Nose Cut one

Eye Cut two >

Attach nose

A   A

Head top
—
Cut one

Attach
ear

Attach
ear

Foot
—
Cut two

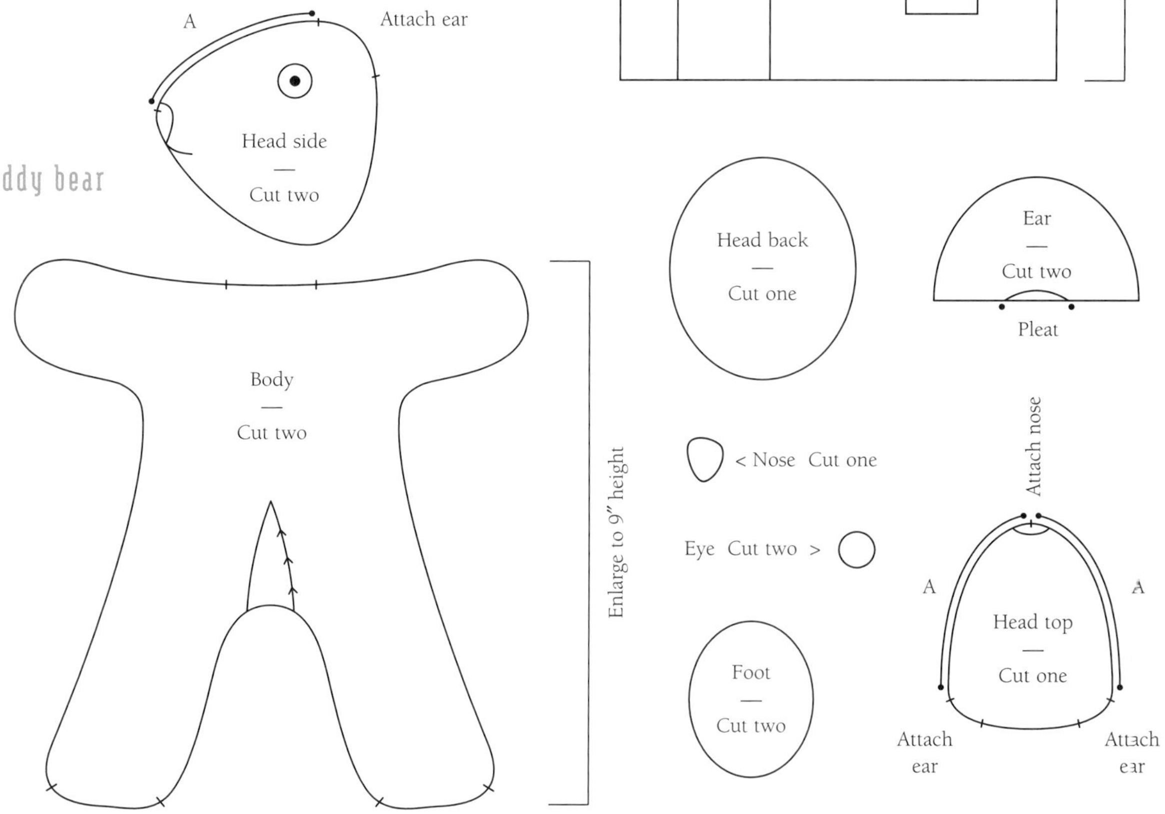

Cut shapes
as needed for
placement

kitty cat pillow

Enlarge to 8 1/4" height

Stencil pattern

Enlarge to 6 1/2" height

wall pocket

Cut one

Enlarge to 16 1/2" height

Fold up along dotted lines
to make tray and front

table runner and napkins

Acorn 2 3/4" length

Leaf 3" length

Border 1 1/2" length

patchwork pillow

Finished patchwork:
19″ length × 13″ height

—

Finished pillow:
18″ length × 12″ height

Enlarge to 19″ length (finished patchwork length)

cross-stitch sampler

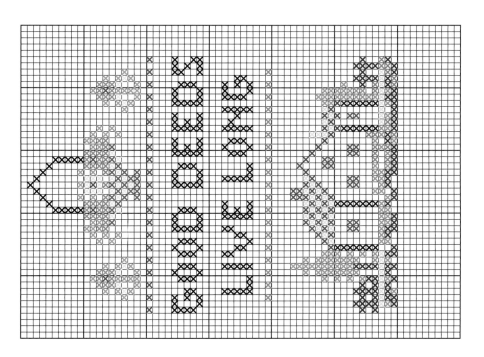

 Finished rug: 37″ length × 28″ height

hooked footstool

Enlarge to 14″ length

papier-mâché dollhouse

easel clock

Ledge back attaches here

Enlarge to 14 1/4" height

Shutter

Enlarge to 3 1/2" height

Door

Enlarge to 4 3/4" height

Window box

Enlarge to 5 1/2" length

Window box

Enlarge to 4" length

Ledge back

Clock Ledge   Fold on dotted lines

Enlarge to 10" length

Easel stand
attaches to
the back of clock
as shown

Fence

Enlarge to 3" height